My Pa
My Destiny

EDWIN L. E. EFERETIN

My Pastor, My Destiny
Copyright 2009 by Edwin Lawrence Ehigiamusoe Eferetin.

For further information or permission, contact:

Lifeway Publishing House
Life Renewal Ministries International
Unit 69 Enterprise Centre
Off Nangor Road,
Parkwest,
Dublin 12
Republic of Ireland

Tel: **01-5540942,**
Fax: **01-5543306**
Mobile: **+353(0)85 1117454, 0872694783**
E-mail: **liferenewal@hotmail.com**
Web: **www.liferenewalministries.org**

CONTENTS

FOREWORD

I am excited that my friend and brother, Pastor Edwin Lawrence Ehigiamusoe Eferetin has written this book that I consider timely and prophetic. God's plan for the end-time church is for the hearts of the children to be turned to their fathers. Pastors are spiritual fathers and they are God's method for the release of miracles here on earth. God has never done anything on earth without human involvement.

Man is the legal authority on earth and has been empowered by God to bring about positive changes here on earth. I believe that this book has come to destroy the diabolical deception that pastors are ordinary men and that they should be treated as such. They carry divine grace for the liberation of humanity from the bondage of Satan. Your value for them will release the flow of what they carry to you.

Pastor Lawrence epitomizes what he has written. His value and respect for men and women of God is legendary. Little wonder why God gave him this awesome revelation that will cause a revolution in the church. As a pastor, I highly recommend that every pastor and church member gets this book.

Thank you, my friend and brother for yielding yourself to God for the release of this book for the benefit of the church and the world.

PASTOR JEFFREY IYONAWAN
MIRACLE ASSEMBLY

DEDICATION

I have always dedicated my life to God the owner and the giver of life. Likewise I wish to humbly dedicate this book to the Almighty God and His beloved Son Christ Jesus my Saviour and my Redeemer.

With gratitude, I would like to dedicate this book of revelation knowledge and power to God Almighty, who inspired and empowered me to write this book.

To my dad, Pa Daniel Ehigiamusoe Evboboru and mum, Mrs. Grace Oyhomwenughae Ehigiamusoe Nee Osunbor of blessed memory. My wife Pastor Helen Eferetin for her great support in the fulfilment of this vision and my divine godly and chosen children Kevin, Jeffrey, Naomi and Iwinosa. I highly appreciate members of Life Renewal Ministries International, for believing in my vision to this dying world. For that I am proud and thankful to you all for your prayers and support.

I want to appreciate my Church Secretary, brother Frederick Ogieva and sister Gbeminiyi Shogunle for proofreading the manuscripts. I want to acknowledge all the great ministers of God on whose shoulders I have stood many times to be inspired.

INTRODUCTION

My Pastor, my Destiny is a book that reveals one of the most untold stories about God's messengers and ministers in the body of Christ. Likewise it is a book that will provoke a mixed reaction to those who will read it. To some it will be a confirmation of the truth that has added colour to their lives or perhaps to some a wake-up call and a realization of the fact that the devil has used them to destroy their own destiny and hinder their success for too long.

It is true that when the purpose of a thing is not known abuse is inevitable. You will discover the true agenda of God's plan concerning Pastors as destiny carriers rather than carriers of the malicious lies of the devil. In this book, I will expose some of the hidden tricks and devices that are employed to hinder believers from the opportunity of receiving their blessing from God.

The reasons we are not seeing the move of God in our churches and communities the way we are suppose to, have been made manifest in this book. A true freedom as we know is nothing but the word of God which has the ability to make anyone free.

In the secular world, doctors, nurses, lawyers and engineers, are well sought after by all whether Presidents, Prime ministers, Kings, Queens, Mayors, Senators or the elites and the non elites in our Community. But Ministers of God are the last person today that most people will turn to. Even when God has empowered his messengers as agents for change, peace, healing, joy, freedom, success, happiness, you name it; yet very few know them.

Others who follow them have misunderstood or have the wrong interpretation of what Pastors truly are. The church is the light for the world to see. Yet so many people's heart and mind have been blindfolded against the messenger of message.

> *"Verily I say unto you, all these things shall come upon this generation. O Jerusalem, Jerusalem, that killeth the prophets, and stoneth them that are sent unto her! How often would I have gathered thy children together, even as a hen gathereth her chickens under her wings, and ye would not! Behold, your house is left unto you desolate."* [MATTHEW 23: 36-38]

Come with me on this mountain of divine revelation in unfolding the most needed plans of God given to men among men, with the supernatural unction to undo all evil manoeuvring of the wicked, in order to release the divine purpose of God for mankind.

Come with me to celebrate life because the glory is here!

CHAPTER ONE

THE PURPOSE OF A PASTOR

'...for the equipping of the saints;' EPHESIANS 4:12

There are many churches.... but few pastors.

Make sure you're not missing God's provision in your life. The agenda of God concerning a man or a woman of God with a special assignment in the body of Christ; is far greater than your own wildest dreams, visions and ambitions. Everything He created is for the realization of his purpose. His purpose is to see us walking in our preordained destiny. The Bible stated that

"... God saw everything that He had made, and indeed it was very good."

It was God's will to see that every good thing he made remains good. God made man with the intent of keeping the good thing He had made on the earth. So Adam being the first representative of the human race lost his God given mandate and ability to function in His purpose. Unfortunately, the good things he made seemingly broke down. Everything seemed to work against God's original purpose. Man began to live for his own selfish ambition and will. Evil entered his mind and corrupted God's creature. The good things God saw became evil. This was against His purpose for creation. The need therefore arose for God to re-equip man in order to know His purpose.

"Surely the Lord GOD does nothing, without revealing his secret to his servants the prophets." **[Amos 3:7]**

God spoke through prophet Amos, in the above Bible scripture that whatever He intends to do on earth either for a nation or a people will be revealed to His messengers. Not only will He reveal His secrets to Prophets but those things revealed will likewise be accomplished through Prophets. We cannot afford to neglect this untold truth in our churches and communities. We should be tired of seeking for solutions from science and technology. Most churches have become historical buildings .Others are simply buildings for ceremonies and social gathering. Churches were supposed to be a house of refuge, solution and God's meeting place for mankind.

God is not a selfish creator. He created the earth to be inhabited by man in order to achieve his desire. He has made his will and he will never change. While the CEO of the big corporation can hire a professional today and within few months he can likewise withdraw his contract. But God cannot terminate or cancel the colourful destiny he has created in you no matter the state or circumstances you may be in. Many employers have fired their employees because of wrong conduct that can put their company in jeopardy. That is man. But God is faithful and good. He did not withdraw Adam from the earth but was still willing to help him to achieve his purpose. Our destiny is paramount to God every single day. His plans towards us are not plans of evil but of good to give us a future that fulfils his purpose.

In God's agenda men and women of God are sent for the equipping of the believers. God's divine help-mate in helping men to fulfil their God's given destiny are Pastors.

There is a speculation about the meaning and the purpose of a Pastor. Some offered their best guesses while others confirm that they just made up a purpose for a pastor. God has not left us in the dark to wonder. We can see God's purpose and will concerning pastors as revealed in his Word. The same is true in discovering God's purpose in fulfilling your destiny. God's word is the true foundation for nations and people to build on. He has not created a nation or a people for a divine purpose without His word - **THE HOLY BIBLE**.

The Bible is very important to nations and people. Here are examples of what few America Presidents have said about the Holy Bible:-

"It is impossible to govern the world without God and the Bible". **GEORGE WASHINGTON**

"The whole inspiration of our civilization springs from the teachings of Christ and the lessons of the prophets. To read the Bible for these fundamentals is a necessity of American life". **HERBERT HOOVER**

"In regard to this great book, I have but to say, it is the best gift God has given to man. All the good Saviour gave to the world was communicated through this book. But for it we could not know right from wrong. All things most desirable for man's welfare, here and hereafter, are to be found portrayed in it."
ABRAHAM LINCOLN

Your destiny was God's plan. Every plan has it outlines ordered. No one can truly discover his destiny in life without turning to God. Everything begins with him. Your life destiny is not self made.

It all started with God. Therefore there is no perfect actualization of your destiny without Him. He is the designer of every destiny. Your life destiny is the reason you were shaped the way you are. As a matter of fact you are in existence because of your God's given destiny. In fact your existence is for the purpose of manifesting this divine destiny. In view of this, there is an order which is required to help you succeed and manifest your destiny. Stop guessing. Your life is too valuable. The absence of light is darkness. Have you felt the absence of light in your life? Congratulations, you're about to manifest a stress free life.

This book in your hand is set to unveil the untold story about God's purpose for Pastors, which is the hidden truth in ministry. This untouched aspect is the true foundation in helping believers to enjoy sweat less success in their pursuit in life and their walk with God.

There are many churches.... but few Pastors. Then He said to His disciples,

"...the harvest is great and the workmen are few." [MATTHEW 9:37]

When a purpose for a thing is not known, abuse is inevitable. There are so many misunderstood and misinterpreted beliefs mostly within the body of Christ. Sincerely speaking, so many Christian have been robbed of their enviable destiny, because their minds have been infected with satanic virus.

The scriptures cannot be broken; it is only the truth you know that has the ability to make you free. The mysteries of the truth about sent men and women amongst us cannot be over emphasized.

> *"O Jerusalem, Jerusalem, thou that killest the prophets, and stonest them which are sent unto thee, how often would I have gathered thy children together, even as a hen gathereth her chickens under her wings, and ye would not"* why because they have reject the sent one among them. Behold, your house is forsaken and desolate."* [MATTHEW 23:37-38]

In the above scripture Jesus, unveiled one major reason why visions, dreams and destinies are hindered, stagnated or completely destroyed. Permit me to use Pastor in this context to represent Prophets, Priests, Bishops, Teachers, Evangelists, etc as the anointed men and women of God.

There is a total desolation to a person or a nation who reject the sent one among them. The sent one is the Pastor; gathering the children of God and helping them to fulfil their destiny and dreams.

Desolation means barren or to lay waste; devastated, deprived or destitute of inhabitants, deserted; uninhabited, having the feeling of being abandoned by friends or by hope. Whatever God has said is not subject to any opposition on earth irrespective of race, colour or profession. Many dreams and visions have been aborted or laid wasted. Many destinies are never fulfilled. Potentials buried, truth never spoken, songs never sang, books never published in-fact messages never preached due to misplacement of priority towards God's purpose and agenda. However the grace and the power of God's love have risen upon you now.

Come with me on this mountain for a divine revelation in unfolding the most needed pre-ordained men of God among men with the supernatural unction to undo all evil manoeuvring of the wicked in order to release the divine purpose of God for mankind.

Understanding is the key that make men outstanding. It is my prayer that you will receive the power of the Holy Ghost to comprehend the hidden treasures for a stress free life.

How can we truly give our life a meaning? How can we take dominion over our destiny and control every situation and circumstance of life? No more, you cannot afford to live your destiny subject to chances and circumstances. You may have done all you know to do but until you apply the right key designed by God; you will never ever have success in giving your life a meaning and thus fulfilling your destiny.

This book aims to reveal God's purpose and agenda for the end time church.

Only the manufacturer or the accredited dealer can reveal or change any faulty parts in order to obtain the maximum functions for the product. Your life is a product of a manufacturer which is God Almighty. In other words your body is a genuine proof of a designer which is God. So living your life without believing the Bible and fully applying his principles is destructive. Our manual for living is the Holy Bible.

Jerusalem represents a city and a people of God. Pastors were sent to them by God from among them. But many of the Pastors were not accepted or received, others were killed or imprisoned. All these happened because the people lacked understanding of the will and purpose of God's agenda over their lives.

Jesus lamented and said;

"How often would I have gathered you together as a hen gathers her chicks under her wings but you wouldn't?"

The truth of this revelation is that every sent Pastor owes God a responsibility in helping the believer to fulfil their destiny. They are destiny carriers.

God cannot do anything without the use of man. Man is God's mouth piece on earth. Human being is God's channel through which He can execute His will on earth. They are the messengers of divine message. Prophets, Priests, Levites are God's agent of old. But today we have Bishop, Evangelists, Pastors etc ordained to give our generation a hope and a future.

"This is that Moses who said to the children of Israel, 'The LORD your God will raise up for you a Prophet like me from your brethren. Him you shall hear.'   [ACTS 7:37]

What are the concepts of God concerning this office and the appointment of Levites, Priests, and Prophets? Well, from the beginning it was not so. It all began after the fall of man in the Garden of Eden. After man lost his dominion to Satan, God's will for mankind to enjoy life and fulfil his destiny was completely destroyed. The hearts of men and women seem stolen from their Father (God).

To this end God had to search for men and women he could use to restore man's destiny.

This book has been written to help mankind rediscover God's master plan for liberating their destinies and dreams that has been shattered. The word of God says you shall know the truth and the truth shall make you free.

"How then shall they call on him in whom they have not believed? And how shall they believe in him of whom they have not heard? And how shall they hear without a preacher? And how shall they preach, except they are sent?"
[ROMANS 10:14-15]

Where is the place of the sent one in our communities and lives?

Where are the prophets like: Moses, Noah, Enoch, Abraham, Samuel, Eli, Daniel, David, Elijah, Elisha, Haggai, Hosea, Ezekiel, Jeremiah, Joel, Zechariah, Joshua, Habakkuk, Isaiah, Jonah, Micah, Apostle Paul, John, Matthew, James, Peter, John the Baptist, Gideon, Barak, Jephthae in our communities and lives today? Beloved, God has not changed. He is the same yesterday, today and forever more.

God used these men at various times in the past to accomplish and fulfil His will and agenda. Why can He not do the same now? God is still in the business of changing our community. He is very much ready as of old to change our lives through his chosen ones among men. If the long expected community changes and destinies of lives are laid upon these men as it were of old; why have we lost the value and the potential of these chosen ones? Why? … Why? …WHY?

Why are these men the major focus of journalists, the media and press? Why has the issue about these anointed men and women become the subject focus of our community at large? Even the so called Christian folks are the main instrument in slandering the Pastors? We have completely misplaced God's purpose and His agenda. We no longer see what we were supposed to see in them.

See the consequences of working against the anointed ones in **2 SAMUEL 1: 21** that are still in effect today in Israel.

"Ye mountains of Gilboa let there be no dew, neither let there be rain upon you, nor fields of offerings for there the shield of the mighty is vilely cast away, the shield of Saul as though he had not been anointed with oil". **[2 SAMUEL 1:21]**

Because of the anointing upon the life of man; the heaven was shut against the mountains of Gilboa from rain, dew and offering till date.

Examining the condition and circumstances of our today's world, leaves us with a feeling like life is out of control. We live in a generation whose plans always go wrong. We buy more but enjoy less. We have multiplied our possessions but reduced our value. We trusted in medicines rather than divine healing. We buy more medicines but less healing. We have invented more medical equipments but less healing and more sicknesses and diseases. We live in days of two or three jobs but more broken homes and poverty.

"If the foundation can be destroyed what can the righteous do?" **[Psalm 11:3]**

We have cleaned up our body, but polluted the soul and the mind. Believe in technology for peace and comfort; but fear and uncertainty is breaking the entire universe. Days of luxurious homes, but more inconveniences; and broken families. We have learnt how to make a living but not a life. We have exchanged truth for lies, desiring the glory of men rather than the glory of God. We trusted in the works of our hands more than the works of God.

We have chosen our way rather than His way.

"My thoughts are not your thoughts neither are my ways your ways saith the Lord of Host." **[ISAIAH 55:8]**

WHO IS A PASTOR?

According to the dictionary definition, Pastor is a noun and it is defined as a Christian minister or a priest who is a leader of a congregation. But according to the word of God, a Pastor is a shepherd; a shepherd is one who leads God's people, which is the church. The Pastor is one who oversees, he leads, he guides, he protects, he teaches, he trains, he counsels, he preaches, he prays and he feeds the church with spiritual food which is the Word of God.

We should understand that the LORD is the good shepherd which David speaks of in the book of Psalms. We should also understand that Jesus declares that he is the good shepherd thus making him God.

"I am the good shepherd: the good shepherd giveth his life for the sheep" [JOHN 10:11]

God said, I will give you a Pastor like Himself. A true shepherd in JEREMIAH 3:15-21

"And I will give you shepherds according to my heart, who will feed you with knowledge and understanding. Then it shall come to pass, when you are multiplied and increased in the land in those days," says the LORD, "that they will say no more, 'The ark of the covenant of the LORD.' It shall not come to mind, nor shall they remember it, nor shall they visit it, nor shall it be made anymore. At that time Jerusalem shall be called The Throne of the LORD, and all the nations shall be gathered to it, to the name of the LORD, to Jerusalem. No more shall they follow the dictates of their evil hearts. In those days the house of Judah shall walk with the house of Israel, and they shall come together out of the land of the north to the land that I have given as an inheritance to your fathers. But I said: 'How can I put you among the children. And give you a pleasant land, A beautiful heritage of the hosts of nations?' "And I said: 'You shall call Me, "My Father," And not turn away from Me.' Surely, as a wife treacherously departs from her husband, So have you dealt treacherously with Me, O house of Israel," says the LORD. A voice

was heard on the desolate heights, weeping and supplications of the children of Israel. For they have perverted their way; they have forgotten the LORD their God.

However, the role of a shepherd (Pastor) which God promises to give has this major heavenly assignment to feed you with knowledge and understandings.

God looked down upon the earth to see how far we are doing in taking dominion and manifesting our fruitfulness. God saw they that have been empowered to dominate being dominated. Then God said in **HOSEA 4:6**

"My people are destroyed for lack of knowledge. Because you have rejected knowledge, I also will reject you from being priest for me; because you have forgotten the law of your God, I also will forget your children."

Pastors are God's shepherd sent to teach the ways of God and His law. To reject a truly sent Pastor means one being rejected by God as a priest. Every believer that follows God sent men and women are priest of God. The answer to several crises in so many lives today is rooted in the working knowledge of God's word. Divine knowledge commands divine power.

Knowledge of the word of God without divine understanding will cause desolation, weeping and pains. Understanding is what made man outstanding in live. A believer that lacks the understanding of the way of the spirit will certainly walk in the congregation of the dead. Spiritual understanding of the written and spoken word of God, easily produce amazing results in life.

A good shepherd of the Lord; stand in the place of God to help people know the truth of the walking power of God. The position of these men and women of God cannot be overemphasized in our communities and lives

This is one of the most important agenda of God in choosing men and women within our communities to accomplish His plans and purpose to everyone who call upon His Name. While others are finding it harder and very difficult to accept this divine order of God, those who know them have little understanding or believe their divine assignments. Pastors are destiny carriers. Shepherd cares, protects, guides, feeds, comforts, restores and also give their life in helping their sheep to fulfil their God's given purpose in life.

Therefore, the answer to life's fulfilment is concealed in the plan of God. Until we value what God values and honour what God honours, life impossibilities remain unchallenged. The fulfilment of destiny is basically upon the revealed truth of the concepts of God's agenda to terminate the human struggle.

Come and I will give you shepherds according to my heart, who shall feed you with knowledge and understanding. [JEREMIAH 3:15]

God has chosen his ministers as instruments of divine change in the affairs of the kingdom of men. Pastors are anointed men among men commissioned with the mandate of fulfilling the plans and the purpose of God for our generation. Ministers of God are destiny carriers and helpers with unction to function in providing direction for men and enabling them to take deliveries of their inheritance in God. There is absolutely no hope of change to our lives and communities, without the divine intervention of God's anointed men.

Surely the Lord GOD will do nothing, but he revealed his secret unto his servants the prophets. [AMOS 3:7]

The prophetic tool is one of the greatest spiritual weapons given to believers in their generation to dominate, rule and take control over their lives without controversy. This is one of the most important concepts given to men to terminate struggles and enjoy sweat less triumph. There is no more begging. Take control of your life now.

To reinforce these prophetic weapons according to his divine power, God has given unto us all things that pertain to life and godliness through the knowledge of him that have called us to glory and virtue.

No more shall they follow the dictates of their evil hearts.

In the above scripture, God admonishes us not to walk in our human feeling or carnal manner of comparing spiritual things with carnal system accepted to the world. Apostle Paul said in **1 CORINTHIANS 1:18**

For the message of the cross is foolishness to those who are perishing, but to us who are being saved it is the power of God.

The preaching of the cross of Jesus Christ seem foolish to those who are perishing but it's the power of God to save as many that believe. Likewise the divine agenda of God in anointing men and women as heaven sent ambassadors to undo the work of the wicked seem childish and unfair in looking onto Pastors as destiny carriers.

Come with me to celebrate life because the glory is here!

Let us look at the meaning of who a Pastor truly is from their assignments.

GOD'S MESSENGER - I will raise them up a prophet from among their brethren, like unto thee; and I will put my words in his mouth, and he shall speak unto them all that I shall command him. **DEUTERONOMY 18:18**.

GOD'S SENT - Come now therefore, and I will send thee unto Pharaoh, that thou mayest bring forth my people the children of Israel out of Egypt.

GOD'S CHOSEN - And the priests the sons of Levi shall come near; for them the LORD thy God hath chosen to minister unto him. **DEUTERONOMY 21:5**.

(ii) And Samuel said to all the people, See ye him whom the LORD hath chosen, that there is none like him among all the people. **I SAMUEL 10:24**.

(iii) Then David said none ought to carry the ark of God but the Levites: for them hath the LORD chosen to carry the ark of God, and to minister unto him for even all the people? And all the people shouted, and said, God save the king. **I CHRONICLE 15:2**.

GOD'S ORDAINED - Before I formed thee in the belly I knew thee, and before thou camest forth out of the womb I sanctified thee; I have appointed thee a prophet unto the nations. **JEREMIAH 1:4**

PASTOR ARE CALLED FOR PERFECTING GOD'S PEOPLE - And he gave some [to be] apostles; and some, prophets; and some, evangelists; and some, pastors and teachers; for the perfecting of the saints, unto the work of ministering, unto the building up of the body of Christ, till we all attain unto the unity of the faith, and of the knowledge of the Son of God, unto a full grown man, unto the measure of the stature of the fullness of Christ:

PASTOR ARE GOD'S GIFT TO THE WORLD - For every high priest, being taken from among men, is appointed for men in things pertaining to God, that he may offer both gifts and sacrifices for sins: Wherefore he saith, When he ascended on high, he led captivity captive, And gave gifts unto men. **EPHESIANS 4:8**

THEY SPEAK THE MIND OF GOD - And I will make a true priest for myself, one who will do what is in my heart and in my mind: and I will make for him a family which will not come to an end; and his place will be before my holy one forever. **1 SAMUEL 2:35**

THEY ANOINTED ONES - The Spirit of the Lord is upon me, because he hath anointed me to preach the gospel to the poor; he hath sent me to heal the broken-hearted, to preach deliverance to the captives, and recovering of sight to the blind, to set at liberty them that are bruised. **LUKE 4:18-19**

THEY ARE SHEPHERDS - and I will give you shepherds according to my heart, who shall feed you with knowledge and understanding. Jeremiah 3:15

THEY ARE SPIRITUAL FATHER - For though ye have ten thousand instructors in Christ, yet have ye not many fathers: for in Christ Jesus I have begotten you through the gospel. 1 Corinthians 4:15

THERE ARE MANY CHURCHES... BUT FEW PASTORS.

Beloved, ask yourself these questions... where would Joshua be without Moses; where would Timothy be without Paul; where would Elisha be without Elijah; where would the nation of Israel be without Moses; where would the disciples be without Jesus. Where would the nation of Israel be without Joshua, Gideon, David, where would you and I be today without Jesus and Jesus representatives who are the true men and women of God who have saved billions of souls today?

Ask the lord to reveal your Pastor unto you. There is great destiny waiting to be explored in you. Do not allow the enemy to waste your colourful destiny. The Lord is in need of you now. Therefore, everything holding your destiny will be destroyed in the name of Jesus. Without the heavenly sent one; life struggle continues. As you prepare yourself to walk unto this divine plan of God, may you remain victorious the remaining days of your life. For by strength shall no man prevail! It is not by might or by power but by my spirit said the Lord of Host. Every mountain of stagnation receives the Holy Ghost destruction in the name of Jesus.

CHURCHES ARE MANY BUT PASTORS ARE FEW.

CHAPTER TWO

GOD'S AGENT FOR DIVINE INTERVENTION

And I will raise me up a faithful priest that shall do according to that which is in mine heart and in my mind: and I will build him a sure house; and he shall walk before mine anointed forever **[1 SAMUEL 2:35]**

And I have raised up for Me a steadfast priest; as in My heart and in My soul he doth do; and I have built for him a steadfast house, and he hath walked up and down before Mine anointed all the days; **[1 SAMUEL 2:35]**

What are divine interventions? These are the acts of God released to cause or change negative circumstances to a positive one. To enhance the fulfilment of purpose, there must be a divine move of the Almighty God in breaking every impossible yoke. Called ministers of God are such divine heaven agents with the mandate to intervene in the affairs of men. Therefore the messenger of God are divinely sent out and put in place to enhance the effective manifestation and a performance of God's will and purpose for this end time. In accordance to God's awesome desire concerning his will, chosen men have become his instruments ordained and commissioned for His purpose and plans on earth. These anointed ones carry the unction to execute the mind of God as heaven's ambassadors on earth.

In **2 Kings 5:9-14** the Bible reveal the experience of the Syrian Captain who was a leper.

Then Naaman went with his horses and chariot, and he stood at the door of Elisha's house. And Elisha sent a messenger to him, saying, "Go and wash in the Jordan seven times, and your flesh shall be restored to you, and you shall be clean. Naaman became furious, and went away and said, "Indeed, I said to myself, 'He will surely come out to me, and stand and call on the name of the LORD his God, and wave his hand over the place, and heal the leprosy. Are not the Abanah and the Pharpar, the rivers of Damascus, better than all the waters of Israel? Could I not wash in them and be clean?" So he turned and went away in a rage. And his servants came near and spoke to him, and said, "My father, if the prophet had told you to do something great, would you not have done it? How much more then, when he says to you, 'Wash, and be clean'? So he went down and dipped seven times in the Jordan, according to the saying of the man of God; and his flesh was restored like the flesh of a little child, and he was clean.

The evidence of darkness in your home while light is shining in your surrounding neighbourhood, is a proof that all is not well in your home. What will you do after hours of self help! You might decide to look out for help.

Finally you call an expert who discover the fault and restore normal power supply to your house. The agenda of God is undoing that unforeseen darkness over us, is by embracing God's anointed men and women around our lives. You were not created to be independent by yourself but to be God's dependant. Do not break the hedge of God upon your life. We are in the latter days, the end time Church shall be established by God on the top of the mountain and all shall flow into it to seek help from God.

> *But in the latter days it shall come to pass, that the mountain of Jehovah's house shall be established on the top of the mountains, and it shall be exalted above the hills; and peoples shall flow unto it. And many nations shall go and say, Come ye, and let us go up to the mountain of Jehovah, and to the house of the God of Jacob; and he will teach us of his ways, and we will walk in his paths. For out of Zion shall go forth the law and the word of Jehovah from Jerusalem.* **[MICAH 4:1-2]**

There are agents of darkness whose sole assignment is to see that no one succeeds in life. So also there are agents of God sent to destroy the work of darkness.

> *"But by a prophet Jehovah brought the people of Israel out of Egypt, and by a prophet were they preserved".* **[HOSEA 12:13]**

Every agent of darkness has an assignment to afflict people's lives by placing barriers, obstacles, hindrances, curses, sickness, poverty and failure in their ways but the agent of God (Pastors) stands in the place of heaven to undo every evil assignment over the destiny of men. What the witch doctor held; God's men can release by the power of God's anointing in them. Whenever light shows-up, darkness must disappear. The glorious light of heaven is lit over you now.

Many respect and accord the witch doctors more honour than the men and women of God that are divine agents to destroy the evil works of these wicked and stubborn witch doctors.

Without controversy anointed men are ambassadors of God's kingdom on earth. Despite the negative views of people about men of God and their credibility; the truth must be said, God's order must not be avoided or despised for any reason. If there is no original there cannot be fake. The foundation of God stands sure; having this seal.

Every ambassador holds the authority to guide and protect every citizen of his country under his domain against unlawful arrest. Ministers of God are heaven ambassador to the citizen of heaven on earth. Also they hold the divine power and authority to nationalize anyone to become heaven citizen. They are licensed, sent and mandated to protect, guide, care, teach and preach the arrival of the kingdom of heaven on earth.

Every power in the negative supernatural that is responsible for the stagnation of lives will be terminated through the anointing of these chosen one of God. Curses of barrenness, failures, setbacks, generational curses will be destroyed with the divine anointing of your Pastor upon your life.

Until the day, believers settle to work in the divine knowledge of God as revealed in our manual of life; (the Bible) we'll keep running after the winds. The truth is that we are sometimes ignorant of Satan's deception. This is the utmost reason why we must devote ourselves to study and apply the precepts of God. The light of knowledge dispels the darkness of deception and ignorance. It is God's will that you are fully equipped with adequate revelation knowledge in order to access your inheritance. Understanding makes man outstanding. Honour and value what God values. This of course is the only true weapon that can destroy the darkness of the wicked ones.

Satan hates the word of God. So he has employed the forces of lies and deception to stand against the truth of God's word. Without spiritual enlightenment of the divine truth of God's instrument, being made available to the body of Christ; all other knowledge is irrelevant. Apart from the revelation of the Spirit of God, no believer can ever find the true light.

We may be a degree holder or a very important personality, but without the help of God we keep asking question concerning the unfair treatment of the world and of life itself. Darkness is the absence of accurate information about the way God has designed the fulfilment of our destiny.

The wickedness of men are responsible for several lives and destinies being destroyed neither by spells, curses, afflictions, bondage prey, captives, yokes, barrenness, stagnation, etc. Therefore God has anointed His minister with the authority to undo all the wicked activities of these forces of darkness. Doctors, science, technology, Politics, degrees cannot and will not take the place of the divine anointing of God upon men.

After the fall of man, God ordained the office of anointed men through which He may minister his way, thoughts, plans and purpose unto man. God ordained his ambassadors from His throne in heaven to the kingdom of men. But from the beginning it was not so. After man lost his dominion to Satan, God's will for mankind to enjoy life and fulfil his destiny was seemingly destroyed. The hearts of men kept doing evil and practicing all forms of wickedness. God adopted the help of some other men to begin to teach his precepts on earth in order to win back the heart of His creature (Man)

To this end God searched for men and women He could use to restore the destiny of mankind.

PROPHETIC ASSIGNMENT

Prophets proclaim the message given to them, as they beheld the vision of God. They are the spokesmen for God; they speak in God's name and by his authority. These chosen ones are empowered to function as the mouth by which God speaks to men and hence what the prophet says is not of human idea or thought but of God.

Prophets were the immediate medium of God in communicating his mind and will to men. The whole word of God may in this general sense be spoken of as prophetic, inasmuch as it was written by men who received the revelation communicated from God, no matter what its nature might be. The great task assigned to the prophets whom God raised up among the people were to preach the gospel to the poor, to heal the broken hearted, bring deliverance to the captives, recovering of dream, visions and destiny. To reprove and correct all forms of immorality and ungodliness of men. To declare the acceptable year of our God.

"And I will give you Pastors according to mine heart which shall feed you with knowledge and understanding" [JEREMIAH 3:15]

Actually a prophet can be an agent in a given situation tasked to accomplish any kind of supernatural works as chosen by God. Where is the place of your Pastor in manifesting your God's given purpose? The mind of your creator has been revealed. I will give you a pastor that will feed you with His knowledge and understanding for sweat less victory.

Do you remember the word of the Lord in **HOSEA** chapter **4:6** which clearly expresses the reason for most believer deadness in manifesting their God given destiny as lack of knowledge? Knowledge is the key to power.

Understanding makes men outstanding. A hilltop is one of the most conspicuous places to build a house. Nothing on a hill is hidden. As long as the house remains on the hill, it is elevated. Your hilltop is your understanding of the manifold works of God. You were created to be outstanding. Outstanding accomplishment is what is called an exploit. From today receive the divine understanding that will enable you exploit the beauty of your colourful destiny in Jesus Name.

May you have an encounter of supernatural understanding of the mind of God that will shine like lightening, causing every hierarchy of darkness to give way to you. Beloved, until you understand; you cannot *"be out-standing"*

> ***"The man that wandereth out of the way of understanding shall rest in the assembly of the dead."*** **[PROVERB 21:16]**

Find out any man at the top of affairs in your community and you will agree with me that understanding elevated him. President Barack Obama became the first black president of the United States of America not because of his degree. Though his colour was seen as barrier but his understanding gave him an edge over his opponents. The secret for one to be outstanding in life, is understanding. Therefore no one is entitled to take his place in life without the knowledge and understanding of the divine agenda of God. When the purpose of a thing is not known, abuse is inevitable. Your Pastor is heaven's agent sent to help you achieve God's purpose. Therefore receive him and appreciate the work of God upon his life. The anointing you refuse or reject cannot bless you. You need your pastor's blessing. What is blessing? It is the supernatural empowerment of God upon you that enables you to succeed. In other words, it is the ability of God upon your ability that empowers you to prosper in life.

> ***"Behold, I set before you this day a blessing and a curse: the blessing, if ye shall hearken unto the commandments of Jehovah your God, which I command you this day"***, **[DEUTERONOMY 11:26-27]**

Why do we go to the doctor, or lawyer or automobile engineers? Why cannot I fix my car whenever it is faulty? It is my car why go to someone else to get my car fixed? No faulty car can be fixed without mechanical knowledge. The greatest battle you can win in life is to value and accept what can add colour and beauty into your life.

He promised you a redeemer and a deliverer whose name shall be Christ Jesus the saviour of man's soul and today needless to say billions of souls have benefited from this divine and unmerited gift. Beloved, stand out on the word of God in giving your destiny the glorious divine beauty it needs through your Pastor.

Many destinies are in bondage today regardless of the fact that provisions have been put in place for their emancipation.

WARNING AGAINST SATANIC DECEPTION

So many dreams and destinies have been robbed while countless others have being destroyed through satanic deception. There are ways that seem right unto a man but the end of such ways brings pains, setbacks and destruction.

The Book of Matthew revealed such ways and manner that brought about desolation to several generations of old. This report of over two thousand years ago has increased tremendously to a state of emergency.

"Therefore, indeed, I send you prophets, wise men, and scribes: some of them you will kill and crucify, and some of them you will scourge in your synagogues and persecute from city to

city, that on you may come all the righteous bloodshed on the earth, from the blood of righteous Abel to the blood of Zechariah, son of Berechiah, whom you murdered between the temple and the altar. Assuredly, I say to you, all these things will come upon this generation." O Jerusalem, Jerusalem, the one who kills the prophets and stones those who are sent to her! How often I wanted to gather your children together, as a hen gathers her chicks under her wings, but you were not willing! for I say to you, you shall see Me no more till you say, 'Blessed is He who comes in the name of the LORD!' [MATTHEW 23:34-39]*

Despite the infallible word of God, the devil has vowed to manipulate the destiny of God's children through deception in turning the truth of God's word into lies. Why are the mindset of many in our communities and churches focusing on talking evil and negative things about Pastors because of the few corruptible ones? This of course is one of the demonic tricks to afflict people's lives and rob them of their blessings.

When you refuse to accept your Pastor as God's divine agent, you become vulnerable to all the wicked manoeuvrings of the devil. When the people of God in the city of Jerusalem neglected and disregarded their Pastor the Bible stated that their houses were desolate. Nothing was working in their lives. They sought for peace but no peace. WHY? They killed the Pastor with all manner of evil talking, lying and rejection.

If the foundations be destroyed what can the righteous do? Foundations are the bedrock for a sustainable future. Destiny built on a wrong foundation is completely a failure. There is no future to any wrong foundation. Only the truth has the capability to enforce total liberation to men and nations

> *Ye mountains of Gilboa let there be no dew, neither let there be rain upon you, nor fields of offerings for there the shield of the mighty is vilely cast away, the shield of Saul as though he had not been anointed with oil.* [2 SAMUEL 1:21]

Because of the anointing upon the life of Saul; the heaven was shut against the mountains of Gilboa from rain, dew and offering. It is too costly beloved when God has specially ordained a Pastor for the total transformation of a people or a city and somewhere along the line they are not received.

The answer to a life of fulfilment is concealed in the plans of God. Until we value what God values and honour what God honours life impossibilities remain unchallenged. The fulfilment of destiny is based upon the revealed truth of the concepts of God's agenda to terminate the human struggle.

God has chosen his ministers as an instrument of divine change in the affairs of the kingdom of men. Pastors are anointed men among men commissioned with the mandate of fulfilling the plans and the purpose of God for our generation. Ministers of God are destiny carriers and helpers. With the mandate of providing direction for men; empowering them to take delivery of their inheritance.

There is absolutely no hope of change to our lives and communities, without the divine intervention of God's anointed men.

THE RICH MAN REQUEST FROM HELL

Abraham made known to us the manifold wisdom of God's order for a change as quoted below.

> *And he said, Father, it is my request that you will send him to my father's house; for I have five brothers; and let him give them an account of these things, so that they may not come to this place of pain. But Abraham said, they have Moses and the prophets; let them give ear to what they say. And he said, No, father Abraham, but if someone went to them from the dead, their hearts would be changed. And he said to him, if they will not give attention to Moses and the prophets, they will not be moved even if someone comes back from the dead.*
> **[LUKE 16:27-31]**

This is a powerful revelation of what is actually going on in our lives. The rich man in hell begged Father Abraham to send Lazarus back to this earth in order that his brother could hear the word of God and believe. Beloved, I hope you are not waiting for someone to come from heaven to preach the word of God to you? If that is what you are truly waiting for; I am glad to announce to you that the heavenly sent ones are already living in our midst. These are the men and women of God anointed and sent by God as destiny carriers. They are Bishops, Pastors, Teachers, Evangelists, etc commissioned by God to undo the barrier, setback, barrenness, demonic attacks and limitations in our lives.

Abraham said, we have Moses and the pastors, let them give ear to them. But if they reject them, they have rejected their success and breakthrough. This is the will and the purpose of God concerning the fulfilment of our lives on earth. Listen to this truth in **ROMANS 3:4** -

> *For what if some do not believe? Will their unbelief make the faithfulness of God without effect? Certainly not! Indeed, let God be true but every man a liar.*

The power for a divine change in man is totally dependent on God's ordained messenger. Father Abraham revealed the truth of God's supernatural agenda for Pastors. Locate the sent one and your heaven will be opened. Mind you, many who have not located theirs are still looking for revival or prophets and crusade meetings for their healing and deliverance. Why? **2 CHRONICLE 20:20** -

> *...Give ear to me, O Judah and you people of Jerusalem: have faith in the Lord your God and you will be saved; have faith in his prophets and all will go well for you. If thou can believe and exercise your faith on the prophetic declaration of your Pastor you will be healed.*

The mystery of a successful life is learning to apply the principle of God concerning us. Your breakthroughs in life are tied to your sensitivity to God's instructions. The instruction you follow determines the future you create. There is a bright future for you through the divine instruction of the anointed one among you.

MOSES RED SEA AND YOUR RED SEA

And the Lord said to Moses, Why are you crying out to me? Give the children of Israel the order to go forward. Pastors always give teachings to show us the way we ought to go in life. Moses heard from God therefore he commanded them to move and as they obeyed, the sea parted into two. As you obey your Pastor's divine leading in your life every red sea will be parted in Jesus Name. Jesus confirmed to us that; he is the way, the truth and the life. The life you sought for is not tied to your job only but to Christ anointing also. Are you weary? Thinking of giving up? There are answers to all life negative situations in Christ Jesus. He said, come unto me all you that labour and are heavy leaden, I will give you rest. Take my yokes upon you and lean on me. Not until we truly turn our face to him with a sincere heart the battle of life will never cease.

A whole nation ended-up in an unusual battle of life. An escape route they were travelling on against the army of Pharaoh suddenly ended at the red sea. This was a battle that could result in losing a whole nation. God asked Moses to speak to the Israelites to move forward. They (Israelites) believed the command of their Pastor Moses. Naturally, asking them to move forward seemed to be an act of total wickedness. But spiritually speaking, it was God's divine escape route for a perfect deliverance. Similarly, this negative view is in our mind hindering us from receiving our men and women of God.

Needless to say that many dreams and visions have been aborted or destroyed. Many destinies never fulfilled.

Potentials buried, truth never spoken, songs never sang, books never published. Simply because they never had a Pastor or they never believed his counsel for the intervention of God over their life. One of my spiritual mentor once said that mathematics is not difficult, if you take time to understand the formula to solve the equation. Life is very simple if also we care to work it out, in accordance to God's plans.

There is no future to a seed that is not planted. Until you are truly planted in the anointing that destroys the yokes of stagnation, the blessings of God will not manifest.

Life is like a seed that has the tenacity and the ability to become a mighty tree, bearing good and precious fruits. But the seed must yield to the soil for his manifestation. Unplanted seed can be devoured by birds, animals, attack by strong wind and all manner of evil.

Without faith it is impossible to please God. Miracle happens through faith. If you had believed your Pastor with the same kind of faith you had at the crusade ground you would have long been delivered from the wicked works of the devil. This of course is the reason why some believers and unbelievers got healed at the crusade ground. Until we begin to have this kind of faith in following Pastors, we will not experience miracle of healing and deliverance from our churches the way it ought to be; let reset our minds. Many times God has used your pastor to release prophetic word to terminate the work of the wicked ones in your life but because your mind has been corrupted, you're still in the same bondage.

Begin to see yourself blessed, healed and delivered from

your church altar through your pastor and your expectation will connect you to divinity and the miraculous becomes the order of the day. If thou can believe all things are possible to him that believeth. Go in this thy might, taste and see that the Lord is good. You have been chosen to show forth the praise of His mighty power and not shame and reproach.

I release the unction of the power of God to undo all the satanic manipulations in your life. You will be celebrated, you must be celebrated. NO MORE SETBACKS.

Whenever you look at you pastor; how do you normally see him or her? What kind of picture do you see?

As a man thinketh in his heart so he is.

Do you see a deliverer or teacher; divine messenger for your divine fulfilment. Pastors how do you see your church members? What kind of a picture do you have? I normally tell my members that the proof of my calling is to see them prosper in spirit, soul and body.

Man of God, see heaven treasures and colourful destiny in the life of your members. Give them your warm heart of love to be able to impact their lives in accordance to your heavenly mandate. You need to pray for the move of the Holy Spirit in your life for without Him you cannot achieve much. Don't' milk them but make them fat in all goodness of life. Let their success and victory become your daily desire.

Do not sell your life unction for a morsel of pottage. It is too dangerous and costly. God watches over you.

"Behold my servant, whom I uphold; mine elect, in whom my soul delighted; I have put my spirit upon him: he shall bring forth judgment to the Gentiles. He shall not cry, nor lift up, nor cause his voice to be heard in the street. A bruised reed shall he not break, and the smoking flax shall he not quench: he shall bring forth judgment unto truth. He shall not fail nor be discouraged, till he has set judgment in the earth: and the isles shall wait for his law. Thus saith God the LORD, he that created the heavens, and stretched them out; he that spread forth the earth and that which cometh out of it; he that giveth breath unto the people upon it, and spirit to them that walk therein: I the LORD have called thee in righteousness, and will hold thine hand, and will keep thee and give thee for a covenant of the people, for a light of the Gentiles; To open the blind eyes, to bring out the prisoners from the prison and them that sit in darkness out of the prison house"   **[ISAIAH 42:1-7]**

Without controversy, the foundation of God remained unchanged. God's elect have been endued with power by the spirit of God to bring judgment to the entire world. This is the reason why Jesus will come again to judge every man. Otherwise, it will be unfair at the judgment seat of God to send anyone to hell if He has not truly appointed men and women as His mouth piece on earth concerning the judgment day.

Saints of God, begin to honour and have respect to the grace of God given to men and women with these liberation mandates to open the blind eyes, to bring out the prisoners from the prison and those that sit in darkness out of the prison house.

This is a faithful saying and worth accepting. The lies of the enemies are to make us ignorant of the truth but thanks be to God who always prepares a way of escape. This is your season to reign and shine. Arise and shine for the glory of thy Lord has risen over you in Jesus Name.

THE ANOINTED ONE AMONG MEN

By the reason of the anointing every yoke shall be destroyed. Jesus the son of God was sent by the Father with a divine anointing to set man free from the stronghold of satanic bondage. Therefore he said, it's not by might nor by power but by the spirit of the Lord.

It shall come to pass on that day That his burden will be taken away from your shoulder, And his yoke from your neck, And the yoke will be destroyed because of the anointing oil.
[ISAIAH 10:27]

Jesus came under a strong and powerful anointing and His fame spread abroad. In **LUKE** chapter **4: 18**, He said *"... the Spirit of the Lord is upon me, because he hath anointed me...."* The people in the synagogue were surprised because they knew Jesus as the son of the Carpenter whose father is Joseph.

Those who have difficulties in accepting Him as the Son of God were completely grounded.

Until the anointing came upon Jesus, his fame never went abroad. No king reigned in Israel without the anointing. Similarly, no prophet stood in his office without it. Obstacles are cleared off; mountains are brought low, and the Red Sea paved way, all because of the anointing upon the man of God. Only the anointing can destroy the yoke, no matter what the yoke is.

How much breakthroughs you experience in life is determined by the level of the anointing upon your life. Jesus charged the disciples not to go witnessing until they were endued with power from on high. Without the anointing, the disciples were incompetent to operate in their offices, likewise the prophets.

Beloved, rise and take your place in God's will and purpose. Hear what Jesus declared in LUKE 4:25-27 -

> *"But I tell you truly, many widows were in Israel in the days of Elijah, when the heaven was shut up three years and six months, and there was a great famine throughout all the land. But to none of them was Elijah sent except to Zarephath, in the region of Sidon, to a woman who was a widow. And there were many lepers in Israel in the time of the prophet Elisha; and none of them was cleansed, but only Naaman the Syrian."*

Why it is that the widow woman of Zarephath was the only one that didn't experience the great recession and credit crunch. She received the anointing upon Elijah with a great faith. To contend with your pastor is to lose in life. You are indirectly contending with an angel sent to effect divine move of God upon your life.

When you despise the man of God, know that it is not him as a person you have despised but the anointing he carries. So many professing believers fear the diabolical men more than the men and women called by God. It is too dangerous to fight the anointed. Whenever you disregard him you disregard your destiny.

Touch not mine anointed and do my prophet no harms. **[PSALM 105:15]**

Today, so many church folks have tied their destiny by plotting against the anointed of God. They never use their mouth to bless the anointing upon their pastor but they talk about Pastor's house, car, clothes, shoes e.t.c. Friends, stop killing your own destiny. Self inflicted curses have denied so many professing Christians the true beauty of God's blessing. The havoc that gossiping and slandering causes to the body of Christ is immeasurable. Countless men of God have been destroyed likewise several churches crippled by the words of few demonized church members.

I want to challenge you from today to start appreciating your pastor. Jesus declares in **MATTHEW 23:37**, *"... that you will not see me again until you said blessed is he who cometh in the name of the Lord".* If there is any error or wrong doing in your pastor's life, you have no right to judge him but to pray for him.

DISCIPLINE YOUR TONGUE

Death and life are in the power of the tongue. **[PROVERB 18:21]**

For Jerusalem is ruined, and Judah is fallen: because their tongue and their doings are against the LORD, to provoke the eyes of his glory. [ISAIAH 3:8]

Therefore as the fire devoured the stubble, and the flame consumed the chaff, so their root shall be as rottenness, and their blossom shall go up as dust: because they have cast away the law of the LORD of hosts, and despised the word of the Holy One of Israel. [ISAIAH 5:24]

The power of life lay in the use of the tongue likewise death and destruction also lay in the power of the tongue.

"How great a forest is set ablaze by such a small fire? And the tongue is a fire, a world of unrighteousness. The tongue is set among our members, staining the whole body, setting on fire the entire course of life, and set on fire by hell. For every kind of beast and bird, of reptile and sea creature, can be tamed and has been tamed by mankind, but no human being can tame the tongue. It is a restless evil, full of deadly poison. With it we bless our Lord and Father, and with it we curse people who are made in the likeness of God. From the same mouth come blessing and cursing." [JAMES 3:6-10]

"The tongue," says James is *"set on fire by hell."* He uses a strong word in this instance. *Gehenna* is the term James used. It speaks of the fire of the pit itself. We are being cautioned that out-of-control speech is capable of unimaginable destruction. Malicious speech or slanderous

accusations are not only demonically inspired, but the devil takes advantage of the opportunities provided through such speeches to afflict the people of God. More saints have been destroyed, more lives ruined, more churches emptied and more devastation in the vineyard of the Lord by angry, malicious and slanderous speech launched against God's chosen people. Take for example the beautiful encounter of Noah in **Genesis** chapter **9**.

THE CURSE OF NOAH UPON HAM

Noah and his children received the blessing of God to refill the universe after the first generation had been destroyed. Noah became drunk to the extent that he fell asleep naked. His first son Ham, saw his father's nakedness and made mockery of him. Canaan went and told his brothers outside their home. When his brothers Shem and Japheth heard about their father's nakedness they quickly took a garment and placed it on the back of their shoulder and covered their father's nakedness. They turned their face backwards so that they didn't see his nakedness. Immediately Noah woke up and having known what happened he placed a curse upon Cannan, Ham's son. The blessing over his life to be the father of the descendant of Canaanites was wiped out by the curse of his father.

Beloved, you can see that it is dangerous to mock and despise God's servant even when they make mistakes. Today there is not a single Canaanite on the surface of the Earth because Ham mocked a man of God.

I believe that some Christians do a far more unwholesome

job of destroying churches and men of God than in helping to build the kingdom of God. Few of us who call the Name of Christ have ever lived up to the responsibilities imposed by the name we bear. Our Lord commanded us to love one another, and though we know the words, we don't know the melody. We still go to church, instead of being the church.

James' concern is that Christians can become more like the world than like the Father. Because we live in a world of evil, without diligence, the people of God will more likely reflect the world in which we live than reflecting Him who is our Father. Throughout, the Word of God are warnings against abusing speech to be avoided against our fellow brethren. Most of our speeches are directly targeted to ruin the men and women sent to us.

Then said they, Come, and let us devise devices against Jeremiah; for the law shall not perish from the priest, nor counsel from the wise, nor the word from the prophet. **[JEREMIAH 18:18]**

For he that will love life, and see good days, let him refrain his tongue from evil, and his lips that they speak no guile. **[1 PETER 3:10]**

DAVID AND SAUL

Tell it not in Gath, Proclaim it not in the streets of Ashkelon - Lest the daughters of the Philistines rejoice, Lest the daughters of the uncircumcised triumph. **[2 SAMUEL 1:20]**

King Saul wanted to kill David in several occasion but couldn't because of the divine hand of God's protection over him. But when the news of Saul death came to David, he didn't rejoice irrespective of the fact that Saul had wanted he dead. But he made the above remarkable statement to the entire nation that his death shouldn't be published for the enemy not to mock them. *"Tell it not in Gath, Proclaim it not in the streets of Ashkelon - Lest the daughters of the Philistines rejoice, Lest the daughters of the uncircumcised triumph".* [2 SAMUEL 1:20]

AARON AND MIRIAM

Some Christians even join the unbelievers in the world to talk about men of God with vicious criticism. They have no solution to their life's problem but they claim to have solution to how the church of God should be run. They have no fear of God in their hearts.

Because of the Ethiopian girl whom Moses chose as a wife, Aaron and Miriam began to talk about Moses simply because, he as a prophet of God failed to marry from their race. God does not permit any mortal man the right to criticize his anointed one. It is too dangerous and too costly to bear. Let's see what happened in the word of God.

"And Miriam and Aaron spake against Moses because of the Ethiopian woman whom he had married: for he had married an Ethiopian woman. And they said, hath the LORD indeed spoken only by Moses? Hath he not spoken also by us? And the LORD heard it. Now the man

Moses was very meek, above all the men which were upon the face of the earth.) And the LORD spake suddenly unto Moses, and unto Aaron, and unto Miriam, Come out ye three unto the tabernacle of the congregation. And they three came out. And the LORD came down in the pillar of the cloud, and stood in the door of the tabernacle, and called Aaron and Miriam: and they both came forth. And he said hear now my words: If there be a prophet among you, I the LORD will make myself known unto him in a vision, and will speak unto him in a dream. My servant Moses is not so, who is faithful in all mine house. With him will I speak mouth to mouth, even apparently, and not in dark speeches; and the similitude of the LORD shall he behold: wherefore then were ye not afraid to speak against my servant Moses? And the anger of the LORD was kindled against them; and he departed. And the cloud departed from off the tabernacle; and, behold, Miriam became leprous, white as snow: and Aaron looked upon Miriam, and, behold, she was leprous. And Aaron said unto Moses, Alas, my lord, I beseech thee, lay not the sin upon us, wherein we have done foolishly, and wherein we have sinned. Let her not be as one dead, of whom the flesh is half consumed when he cometh out of his mother's womb. And Moses cried unto the LORD, saying, Heal her now, O God, I beseech thee. [NUMBER 12: 1-13]

If there is anything in life that can stir any hope in our community; it is the hope we have in Christ Jesus. The problem with so many believers is their running mouth. If a ministry is prospering they are annoyed and bitter. Satan will hire them to tie their own destiny by themselves by working against the anointing of God upon the man or the woman of God. If a ministry is not prospering so many also begin to talk about the anointed one.

Get this truth: the very moment you begin to despise a prophet of God in your heart; that is the moment you remove your life from God's anointing covering your life.

In the negative supernatural, what the witches and wizards tie can only be loosed in the positive supernatural through the anointing of God upon a prophet. Do not behave like Miriam and Aaron who spoke against their destiny carrier. You cannot speak against prophets because you did not call them. The God that called them will judge or speak about them.

> *Who art thou that judges another man's servant? To his own master he standeth or falleth. Yea, he shall be holden up: for God is able to make him stand.* **[ROMANS 14:4]**

God will rebuke you by himself if you choose to speak evil against his servant that stand day by day before Him. Listen! Do you have any moral or legal right to judge another man's child to his father? This is not fun! The prophet has nothing to do by himself even if he hears all the evil things spoken against him; but God has so much to do because of His servant who you have despised before Him. With the same measure you mete; God shall measure back to you. Do not be deceived God is not mocked. Whatsoever a man sowed that shall he reaps. Beloved, what have you been sowing recently? Repent today and be delivered in Jesus Name.

When you are chastised by the church leaders you got angry. When you are reproved from your wrong doing you get bitter about the man of God. Whenever we reject the correction of men of God, we have rejected the correction of God. A Christian that has no one to correct him when he is heading for total destruction is void of a spiritual father. When you were disciplined why did you leave the church? To leave a Church when you are under discipline is a curse. How then can you succeed? For by strength shall no man prevail? To speak against a man of God is to challenge the angels attach to his anointing for battle. One of the major causes of generational curses is disregarding God's prophet of old and never believes in them.

Miriam left the presence of God with leprosy and would have remained so till death if not for Moses intervention. But they mocked the messengers of God, and despised his words, and rejected his counsels, until the wrath of the LORD arose against his people, till there was no remedy. **2 CHRONICLES 36:16**

THE COST OF NEGLECTING THE WAYS OF GOD

"Turn you at my reproof: behold, I will pour out my spirit unto you, I will make known my words unto you. Because I have called, and ye refused; I have stretched out my hand, and no man regarded; But ye have set at nought all my counsel, and would none of my reproof: I also will laugh at your calamity; I will mock when

your fear cometh. When your fear cometh as desolation, and your destruction cometh as a whirlwind; when distress and anguish cometh upon you. Then shall they call upon me, but I will not answer; they shall seek me early, but they shall not find me: For that they hated knowledge, and did not choose the fear of the LORD: They would none of my counsel: they despised all my reproof. Therefore shall they eat of the fruit of their own way, and be filled with their own devices. For the turning away of the simple shall slay them, and the prosperity of fools shall destroy them. But whoso hearkened unto me shall dwell safely, and shall be quiet from" fear of evil. [PROVERB 1:23-33]

The way of God seems too simple that many of us think that it cannot save or truly help any man to have a turn around. If we continue to refuse the counsel of God and despise His agenda concerning our life, we will be left to our own way but if we turn to walk in his purpose then he will bless us.

As David and his party passed Bahurim, a man came out of the village cursing them. It was Shimei, the son of Gera, a member of Saul's family. He threw stones at the king and the king's officers and all the mighty warriors who surrounded them! Get out of here, you murderer, you scoundrel!" he shouted at David. The Lord is paying you back for murdering King Saul and his family; you stole his throne and now the Lord has given it to your son

Absalom! At last you will taste some of your own medicine, you murderer! Why should this dead dog curse my lord the king? Abishai demanded. Let me go over and strike off his head!" "No!" the king said. "If the Lord has told him to curse me, who am I to say no? My own son is trying to kill me, and this Benjaminite is merely cursing me. Let him alone, for no doubt the Lord has told him to do it. And perhaps the Lord will see that I am being wronged and will bless me because of these curses. So David and his men continued on, and Shimei kept pace with them on a nearby hillside, cursing as he went and throwing stones at David and tossing dust into the air. The king and all those who were with him were weary by the time they reached Bahurim, so they stayed there awhile and rested. **[2 SAMUEL 16:5-13]**

Shimei is the kinsman to King Saul whom God rejected as a king because of his disobedience and David was the shepherd boy, chosen by God to take the seat of the King of Israel. Because Shimei knew David too well he did not receive him because of his belief that Saul has not actually sinned against God. Shimei's negative attitude shows disrespect for the man of God but more than that Shimei's attitude shows a lack of respect for God! Every day, most of us believer's display attitudes that doesn't regard the chosen one and so also that lacks respect for God.

WAYS WE DISRESPECT

Isn't it strange how big a 20Euro bill looks in the offering basket and how small it looks at the gas pump? Isn't it strange how hard it is to witness to someone but we can tell a dirty joke? Isn't it strange how big 2 hours seems at church and at the movie you don't care about the time? Isn't it strange how hard it is to find words to pray, but when you are talking about others there are plenty of words?

Isn't it strange how hard it is to read your Bible, but that magazine and Romance book is easy? Isn't it strange how quickly your priorities about the church can be bumped by a football game? Isn't it strange how we doubt what the Bible says, but believing everything in the newspaper?

IT SEEMS SO STRANGE DOESN'T IT?

CHAPTER THREE

LIBERATION MANDATE

"And the LORD said, I have surely seen the affliction of my people which are in Egypt, and have heard their cry by reason of their taskmasters; for I know their sorrows".

[EXODUS 3:7]

Israel was under the yoke of slavery and bondage in Egypt for 430 years. Their predicament was beyond any human comprehension. The darkest moment in a man's life is when he is under attack without knowing what to do. Knowledge lies at the heart of the struggle for freedom. You may have done all you know how to do, until you do the right thing, your struggles and pains continues. Whenever Israel sought for freedom through human effort they in return invoked the wrath and anger of their taskmasters. Deceptive human manipulation and trickery for freedom is too costly. Stop deceiving yourself. You cannot afford to end up incurring more pains and afflictions year after year. Locate your prophet so that you can enjoy a sweat less victory. For by a prophet Israel was delivered, and by a prophet they were preserved.

Life is spiritual. Every happening in the physical has its root in the spirit realm. God made man in His image and likeness. God is three persons in one. God the father; God the Son and God the Holy Ghost. Man, made in God's likeness and also has the nature of God. The components that make up a man is three. Spirit, soul and body. Until we come to the understanding of the spirituality of life we will never have victory from the power of darkness.

A nation or people who lack the knowledge of the positive supernatural will live to remain in the congregation of the dead. It is a shocking situation that Christians have abandoned the pastoral liberation unction upon the unusual men among men.

It is interesting to note that, without God's ordained men and women there is no freedom.

> *The spirit of the Lord is upon me because he hath anointed me to preach the gospel to the poor; he hath sent me to heal the broken-hearted, to preach deliverance to the captives and recovering of sight to the blind, to set at liberty them that are bruised. To preach the acceptable year of the Lord.* [LUKE 4:18-19]

When Israel cried to God in prayers, God heard their cry but their situation remained the same.

> *"And God said, Truly, I have seen the grief of my people in Egypt, and their cry because of their cruel masters has come to my ears; for I have knowledge of their sorrow. And I have come down to take them out of the hands of the Egyptians, guiding them out of that land into a good land and wide, into a land flowing with milk and honey; into the place of the Canaanite and the Hittite and the Amorite and the Perizzite and the Hivite and the Jebusite. For now, truly, the cry of the children of Israel has*

come to me, and I have seen the cruel behavior of the Egyptians to them. Come, then, and I will send you to Pharaoh, so that you may take my people, the children of Israel, out of Egypt. And Moses said to God, Who am I to go to Pharaoh and take the children of Israel out of Egypt. And he said, truly I will be with you; and this will be the sign to you that I have sent you: when you have taken the children of Israel out of Egypt, you will give worship to God on this mountain. And Moses said to God, when I come to the children of Israel and say to them, The God of your fathers has sent me to you: and they say to me, what is his name? What am I to say to them"? [Exodus 3:7-13]

God declares to us in His word that He has seen the affliction and the sorrows of his people by the reason of their taskmaster. Yet their bondage and pains still continued. Despite God's readiness and willingness to save them; why would their story remain unchanged even when heaven has signalled their release from the hands of their enemies?

There is absolutely no escape route to any nations or mortal man who is under the yokes of demonic bondage. Science with all his human input and technology will always fail. Doctors and doctors of law need the divine mandate of God for their liberation. The only way to undo and challenge all the forces of darkness is through the release of the supernatural power of God. For 430 years the nation of Israel suffered shame and depression from the forces of darkness in Egypt.

Beloved there is a way of escape from the financial credit melt down that the world is suffering from right now. Turn to God and walk with him through the counsel of his word. If we fail, He said he will laugh at our calamity.

"But ye have set at nought all my counsel, and would none of my reproof: I also will laugh at your calamity" **[PROVERB 1:24]**

Friends, it's time to see and understand the channel through which God effects His change in the affairs of men. God has seen your sorrow and grief now it is your turn to be delivered from the power of the forces of the enemies. God's word cannot work for you but work through you. Until we act upon the declaration of God's word, we are not guaranteed true fulfilment.

Until God located Moses concerning the prayer and fasting of the children of Israel; their bondage remained. God has sent your destiny carrier, his chosen one the messenger and mouth piece of God to launch your destiny for the manifestation of His glory and for your blessing. Arise and shine for the glory of the Lord has risen upon you.

May be of a truth, you have passed through or you are still in this kind of calamity. Israel was looking unto heaven for answer while heaven (God) was looking on earth for a man to use. God keeps using earthly vessels to accomplish his supernatural works on earth. God's divine liberation mandates to save, heal or deliver his children on earth are through human agent. Until Moses was called out and sent by God to the Israelites in the land of bondage they were still living their life at the will of their enemy.

God answers prayer by sending true anointed minister into our lives to help us receive his divine touch.

Your ways are not God's ways neither are your thought God's thought. Don't limit God through your corrupt or polluted thoughts. There is nothing too hard or difficult for God to do. If He could create the whole world from nothing then He can use the foolish things in the eye of the world to confound the mighty and the wise things.

HE IS GOD OF ALL POSSIBILITIES

God is not a man that He should lie, neither the son of man that He should repent, if He says it, that settles it.

> *"I ask then, did God reject his people? May it never be! For I also am an Israelite, a descendant of Abraham, of the tribe of Benjamin. God didn't reject his people, which he foreknew. Or don't you know what the Scripture says about Elijah? How he pleaded with God against Israel."Lord, they have killed your prophets, they have broken down your altars; and I am left alone, and they seek my life." But how does God answer him? "I have reserved for myself seven thousand men, who have not bowed their knees to Baal."* [ROMANS 11: 1-5]

God will never forsake you but He is ever willing to make you the head and never the tail. Why do people feel that God has rejected them? Because they have rejected the prophet of destiny and broken the altar in believing the world system rather than the word of God.

All things are yours. All things are possible. You are welcome to your season for divine possibilities. A two fold cord is not easily broken. As you accept God's prophesy through Elijah, the reserved destiny carrier, among men and women of God may you discover and recover all the good plans of God in your life. God said I know the plans that I have for you; plans of good and not of evil. From today all the evil plans in your life ceases to function in Jesus name.

The God of surprises, yes He is. May He surprise you now! His ways are higher than our ways and His thoughts than our thoughts. The man or the woman of God whom men neglected, despised, and rejected could be the sent one for you. David was a forgotten and despised man but GOD approved of him. Friends, all you need right now is just to believe God's divine arrangement for you. If thou can believe all things are possible to him that believeth. Believe the Lord God and you will be established; believe His prophet and you will prosper. Your hour for the world to celebrate your divine prosperity has come. Your coronation becomes your fulfilment. You were born to reign with Christ.

Never, ever despise the word of God. His word is the master key to unlock every closed destiny. Don't give up on yourself. It is not over until you win!

MOSES LOCATED

God is not a magician! He is a God of orderliness, who honours his word. The word of God is the power of God that works the miraculous. Do you want to shine and reign in life? Locate a minister of God sent and anointed, and you will smile all the rest of your life.

Moses tried to help the Israelites to fight their oppressors one day, only to end-up endangering his life. You may fight and win any life battle but only for a while. If at all you do, how long can you preserve the victory? For by strength shall no man prevail? Let God fight your battles. Position yourself, believe and fully apply God's standard and principles. Then be rest assured that it is settled.

His word declares; for without me ye can do nothing. Moses has to run away from Egypt. From his own people whom, for their sake he rejected the riches of Egypt. He refused to be called son of Pharaoh's daughter. He chose to suffer with the people of God, his brethren.

Moses trying to fight for Israel by flesh almost cost him his life. Human intellect cannot stop the unseen forces of the wicked ones. Either can common sense or carnal weapons of war destroy the thick darkness of barrier, stagnation or satanic devices of the enemy?

Human logic cannot destroy satanic forces. I think you have struggled long enough. It is not about what you think or feel; it is what God says. I think you have struggled enough, you have worked hard enough, and you have endured that failure enough. It is your time to be celebrated. Friends, God's word and His miracles are still the same yesterday, today and forever.

Life in itself is full of impossibilities. The spirit realm is more real than the physical realm. Oftentimes most negative manifestations in the natural have their root in the spiritual realm. So, we will require the unction of the anointing of God to go through.

Due to lack of spiritual knowledge and God's supernatural way of liberation, so many lives, career and destinies are in limbo.

What will the situation of Israel be if they had rejected Moses coming to them as a prophet? Because, this is Moses whom they knew very well as

1. A stutterer
2. A murderer.
3. A failure

How could it be that, the same person that has tried to help before but narrowly escape death? This of course led him to become a refugee in order to save his own life, from the hands of Pharaoh. Moses tried to be a deliverer of his kinsmen but ended up not being able to protect his life in Egypt. Think about this!

"... for by strength shall no man prevail.
[1 Samuel 2: 9b]

Then he answered and spake unto me, saying, this is the word of the Lord unto Zerubabel, saying, not by might nor by power, but by my spirit, saith the Lord of hosts. [Zechariah 4:6]

Beloved, the scripture cannot be broken, I strongly believe in my spirit that your season of refreshing and perfect rest has come in Jesus name. Your moment to prevail over all negative circumstances and situations through the spirit of God upon your life has come.

Moses who ran from Egypt came back with the spirit of God. The death sentence or warrant upon his life couldn't stop him because the anointing of God upon him has erased the death sentence and barrier.

> *And the LORD said, I have surely seen the affliction of my people which are in Egypt, and have heard their cry by reason of their taskmasters; for I know their sorrows and I am come down to deliver them out of the hand of the Egyptians, and to bring them up out of that land unto a good land and a large, unto a land flowing with milk and honey; unto the place of the Canaanites, and the Hittites, and the Amorites, and the Perizzites, and the Hivites, and the Jebusite.* **[Exodus 3:7-8]**

If God says a thing so it is. God said and I am come down to deliver them out of the hand of the Egyptians. We know that the scriptures cannot be broken. God cannot lie. Did He really come down as a person, YES! How? Where? When? Whenever God sent a man with His divine assignment, please know of a truth that God has come down.

> *"Come now therefore and I will send thee unto Pharaoh that thou mayest bring forth my people the children of Israel out of Egypt."* **[Exodus 3:10]**

God's plan is to restore His original purpose and agenda. Therefore receive deliverance from bondage and divine blessing to possess the land of Canaan. In a practical sense, God declared to have heard and answered Israel. God declared that He has come down to deliver his people. He announced His arrival on earth through a man (Moses) whom He sent to Pharaoh. The next thing we discovered in the above scripture is absolutely amazing; that God had to call a man with this liberation mandate to bring forth His people from the hand of their tormentor (Pharaoh). Preparing them also to worship and serve Him as their only true God, with abundance of blessings.

Now, is it right for man to take the place of God you may want to ask? Yes! He has chosen to use earthly vessels sanctified to fulfil His will and desires. So where is your Moses? Have you found him? I mean your God sent deliverer, destiny carrier. Even Jesus, though he was the son of God but he came to the earth like everyone of us. Jesus said to Philip if you have seen me you have seen the father. And also he said to his disciples as the father has sent me so also I have sent thee.

Moses on the other hand couldn't understand this mystery because it is beyond human comprehension. Moses said who am I that I should go to Pharaoh? Behold, when I come unto the children of Israel and shall say unto them, the God of your fathers hath sent me unto you and they shall say to me, what is his name? What shall I say unto them? And God said unto Moses, I AM THAT I AM.

For God to reveal His name to Moses as "I Am That I Am" has a deep mystery that so many people in the body of Christ have no knowledge about. In fact, this is the major reason why many men and women of God have been taken lightly. By that name God is saying He can become anything He wants to become in order to fulfil His will and desire in our lives. Moses tried rejecting the call of God upon his life because of his physical disability. Have you rejected a man or a woman of God sent for your liberation? Why? …colour, race, sex, tribal, non-educated or not having a big church, not wealthy, not politically connected in the community become an issue to so many people. Saints of God, have we forsaken the word of the lord which said we walk by faith not by sight? Sight is a function of your emotion, taste, feeling and smell. while faith is the path of the spirit that leads to life's fulfilment. To be carnally minded is death but to be spiritually minded is life and peace.

Despite Moses familiarity with his people, and having failed before trying to deliver them; his people still accepted and believed in him. They never underrated him. Their confidence in him was very strong. They supported him throughout the various plagues that never actually saved them. They honoured him, respected him, and listened to him. They believed God as well as His mouth piece (Moses).

God wrought several fearful and terrible plagues through the hand of Moses but Pharaoh refused to let Israel go. Each time Pharaoh refused God's liberation mandate through Moses, Pharaoh in return increased his wrath and anger against Israel. The consequences were that their taskmasters had to increase their labour and sufferings.

Supposing it is today's church that a pastor declares those liberation mandate of signs and wonders like Moses did; and at the end of each sign, the people's freedom was denied and subsequently incurred much more sufferings and pains, thank God you can judge for yourselves what would have happened?

Despite the heavy yokes and sufferings Israel incurred because of their Pastor (Moses) whose liberation mandate failed several times yet; the Israelites kept believing in him with all due honour as God's sent. They never complained, nor doubted his calling as God's messenger. The day you give up on your Pastor, which means you have given up on your destiny. When it comes to a situation that you no longer believe or act upon the instruction of your pastor that is where you finally miss it. Moses faithfully and sincerely carried out all the spoken words of God without winning the battle for Israel's freedom.

The man of God (Moses) came on a particular day and declared to the Israelites; thus says the Lord, tonight is your Passover night, therefore let every house buy a lamb according to their family size to sacrifice unto their God and put the blood upon the lintel of their houses because He (God) will visit the land of Egypt to night to smite every first born in the house of their oppressor. May God visit the house of your enemies tonight in Jesus name Amen. Whatsoever is holding your destiny will receive heaven's judgment from now. By the reason of the anointing the yokes of stagnation are broken. Arise and shine for the glory of God has risen upon you.

Without controversy, their obedience destroyed slavery that lasted for 430 years. If only you can believe all things are possible to them that believeth. Surprisingly, no man from amongst them ever complained. With all humility everyone bought their Passover lamb in accordance to the word of the man of God.

Israel saw the unction of God upon Moses hence they could believe him and his word. Have you seen the unction upon your pastor? Is it heaven's unction or earthly unction? Are you there because he is your kindred man or because of the physical assistance or the pride of just belonging to that beautiful cathedral?

The most needful thing in one's life is to carry an unusual anointing. Mary the mother of Jesus told the servants serving at the wedding in Cana of Galilee saying, whatsoever he said to you, DO IT.

Beloved, stop destroying your destiny. Seek God's way and you will be delivered. When you locate the anointing, do not make mockery of it because the anointing you despise cannot bless you.

Pastors are God's ordained men and women sent as heaven's agents to cause supernatural liberation to the dying world. Ignorance of this truth has destroyed and shattered dreams and ruin cities through all ages.

Jesus said whosoever receives you receives me and whosoever rejects you rejects me. Beware, you may be neglecting and rejecting your victory by your careless attitude towards men of God. Locate your minister through whom your God has come down for your sake; as it was in the day of Moses when every force responsible for their captivity was broken.

Israel thoroughly believed God and his prophets. Do you thoroughly believe God and your Moses?

And they rose early in the morning, and went forth into the wilderness of Tekoa: and as they went forth, Jehoshaphat stood and said, Hear me, O Judah, and ye inhabitants of Jerusalem;

Believe in the LORD your God, so shall ye be established; believe his prophets, so shall ye prosper. [2 CHRONICLES 20:20]

Until we see men and women of God as God sees them, we may not provoke the anointing of God in them that destroys yokes. See your ministers as God does. Prophets are spiritual fathers. It is not about them as a person it is the anointing of God. Listen, the heavenly treasure hidden in your life will begin to manifest from now in Jesus Name. If thou can believe, all things are possible to him that believeth.

And by a prophet (Pastor) the Lord God saved Israel and by a Prophet they were preserved. **HOSEA 12:13**

Beloved you are a creature of destiny and purpose. Truly, you are special, unique and uncommon. About six billion people live on this planet; no one has the same DNA composition as you. You are born to reign. You are not living on the planet by accident.

Beloved, declare sincerely in your heart that you believe the word of God. God is in the process of making something colourful out of your life from today. You are in God's agenda right now for success.

Whosoever despises the word shall be destroyed **[Proverb 13:13]** paraphrased. Your prosperity is connected to your prophet. That is why your pastor is your destiny.

You can never have what you hate or despise. If you hate prosperity you will never prosper. Honour prophets and believe them for God said so. The promise of honouring the anointing upon them is the mystery for triumphant living.

Yet he sent prophets to them, to bring them again unto the LORD; and they testified against them: but they would not give ear. [2 Chronicles 24:19]

If we believe doctors and confidently give our body to them to diagnose, so also we should trust God our maker, the giver of life to give us His abundant life through his prophets.

You may say there are some fake and counterfeit prophets. Yes! That is absolutely true but not the whole truth. The fact that you receive a fake currency note doesn't mean that all currency notes are fake. So then you have to carefully check any other currency note to see if it's genuine or fake. The word of God implores us to test every spirit.

How to Know Fake Pastors

Beloved, you may not know a tree by his leaves, but by the fruits it bears. You cannot know the sent men and women of God by the gift without the fruit they bear. God is holy and there is no unrighteousness in him. Satan can give gifts to people but the fruits he bears are always evil.

Beloved, believe not every spirit, but try the spirits whether they are of God: because many false prophets are gone out into the world
[I John 4:1]

In this kingdom, whatsoever the King bids you, go and do. If it is not as commanded, you are on your own.

HEAVEN'S AMBASSADORS TO THE WORLD

Just as the world system used to appoint their official representatives of government to other countries; so also we do in the kingdom of God.

God have his ministers appointed as ambassadors and envoys to represent His interest on earth. Prophets of God can decree a thing in accordance with heaven's law and it shall be established. God chooses to communicate his kingdom's agenda and order through his personal representatives. Truly appointed men and women of God, never speak their personal opinions, but only the official polices of the kingdom which is the Bible.

I have found God's word that said *"And by a prophet the Lord God delivers Israel and by a prophet they were preserved."*

Until you believe the word of God which is the power of salvation, you will never enjoy the blessings of God

> *Come now therefore, and I will send thee unto Pharaoh, that thou mayest bring forth my people the children of Israel out of Egypt. And Moses said unto God, Who am I, that I should go unto Pharaoh, and that I should bring forth the children of Israel out of Egypt?*
> **[EXODUS 3:10-11]**

Here is the hidden mystery most believers and the heathen cannot comprehend. It is written, my ways are not your ways neither are my thoughts your thoughts. Indeed God has come down to deliver his people (through his chosen men). This has been God's plan from the time Adam and Eve disobeyed him.

The scripture cannot be broken. God's way is not subject to any vote or human opinions. For ever O Lord thy word is settled. Believe and save your soul. The devil is wicked and never seeks the good of any except to steal God's word from the heart of men.

His deceptive power is to exchange good for evil, truth for lie which results to fear and doubts. The absolute plans of heaven are revealed now for your total deliverance, healing and prosperity. All these blessings have been entrusted to the care and charge of God's ministers.

> *How God anointed Jesus of Nazareth with the Holy Ghost and with power: who went about doing good, and healing all that were oppressed of the devil; for God was with him.*
> **[ACTS 10:38]**

Jesus was a great high priest and a prophet. The unction of God upon his life is to release good to men and women; in liberating men from the hands of their captors and oppressors.

BELIEVE IT AND BE FREE

Your destiny and success in life is rooted in your belief. Listen, if you have a negative belief about something that is significant for the fulfilment of your destiny; it could keep you from taking the necessary steps for that success to be achieved. Our belief forms the foundation of who we are. Out of the abundance of the heart the mouth speaks.

Choice, actions and decision made in life should be in agreement with the word of God. Heavens and earth shall pass away but my words shall not pass away.

> *And he went out from thence, and came into his own country; and his disciples followed him. And when the Sabbath day was come, he began to teach in the synagogue: and many hearing him were astonished, saying, from whence hath this man these things? And what wisdom is this which is given unto him, that even such mighty works are wrought by his hands? Is not this the carpenter, the son of Mary, the brother of James, and Joses, and of Juda, and Simon? and are not his sisters here with us? And they were offended at him. But Jesus said unto them, a prophet is not without honour, but in his own country, and among his own kin, and in his own house. And he could there do no mighty work, save that he laid his hands upon a few sick folk, and healed them. And he marveled because of their unbelief. And he went round about the villages, teaching.*
>
> **[MARK 6: 1-6]**

There are so many miracles recorded in the ministry of Christ Jesus. He was anointed and sent by God. Unfortunately, He couldn't perform more miracles in his own town. The question we need ask is why? Whenever we fail to honour and value the anointed ones among men for any human or logical reason, we never benefit from that anointing. If you accept a man of God by believing in your heart that God has sent him to you; no power can stop you from receiving your miracle. Anointing despised never blesses. It is too dangerous to stand against the chosen ones.

JESUS WAS ANOINTED FOR LIBERATION

The Spirit of the Lord is upon me, because he hath anointed me to preach the gospel to the poor; he hath sent me to heal the broken-hearted, to preach deliverance to the captives, and recovering of sight to the blind, to set at liberty them that are bruised   Luke 4:18

Jesus was sent and anointed by God as a destiny carrier for mankind. Many despised him while he was here physically over two thousand years ago. Let us come to the knowledge of the truth there is no other way for man's freedom on earth except in God's agenda for man. The facts that so many have also called themselves without heaven's unction over them; should not give anyone room for satanic deception.

Some were expecting Jesus to come in a different body from what we were already used to. ASK FOR THE GIFT OF GOD and save your energy. Your seasons to reign and shine have come.

CHAPTER FOUR

GOD'S AGENT OF CHANGE

And Elijah the Tishbite, who was of the inhabitants of Gilead, said unto Ahab, as the Lord God of Israel liveth, before whom I stand; there shall not be dew nor rain these years, but according to my word.   **[1 KINGS 17:1]**

At a time when booted warriors are trampling under foot all that civilized men held sacred and the anchors of faith are dragging in the storm, the prophets speak a commanding word. They speak of God and conscience, they denounce the vested evils, the mighty and the powerful forces to effect a change at God's will.

Thank God for his prophet that he has appointed as agent of divine change in the affairs of men. This world would have become unbearable if the wicked acts of the evil ones go unchallenged. King Ahab's national shame of demonic idol worship came to an alarming stage; oppression, injustice, immoral religions etc.

King Ahab stretched far before those who have eyes to see; they speak of a new heaven and a new earth to those who have the imagination to perceive. In an age when nations are snarling at each other across every frontier, when races are at each other's throats, and classes are in conflict, Elijah came against King Ahab.

By the will of God through the prophet degree, Elijah withheld rain from the land. What the herbalist or voodooist is to the unsaved, is what men of God are to the believers. The wicked will keep on doing wickedness if there is no superior power to challenge them.

The only way of escape for your destiny trapped by principalities and powers is concealed upon God's true ambassador. Elijah came on the scene to terminate and overthrow all the evil prophets of Baal and subdue them.

God is totally committed to his prophet. He can do nothing on earth without revealing to His servant the prophet.

Do you need a change in your financial predicament or other areas of need within your household? Go to your pastor for he is the only divine connection for a change right now. Your prosperity lies in your obedience to the word of God and your pastor. This is God's standard and principle of doing things.

And by a prophet the Lord brought Israel out of Egypt, and by a prophet where they preserved.
[HOSEA 12:13]

Israel was in captivity for 430 years. When they cried unto God for a change, He sent a man to them in the person of Moses being one of His ordained prophets. God is always good. His good plans are concealed in men and women that so many of us have despised and neglected. This is the day of good things. Every man has a destiny to accomplish, but there are forces that have vowed to work against this. By the divine encounter every evil force working against your blessing will be terminated in Jesus Name

At any time Satan decides to attack lives or nations he employs the office of his evil and wicked agents.

CREDIT CRUNCH DELIVERANCE TO A WIDOW

Arise, get thee to Zarephath, which belongeth to Zidon, and dwell there: behold, I have commanded a widow woman there to sustain thee. So he arose and went to Zarephath. And when he came to the gate of the city, behold, the widow woman was there gathering of sticks: and he called to her, and said, fetch me, I pray thee, a little water in a vessel, that I may drink. And as she was going to fetch it, he called to her, and said, bring me, I pray thee, a morsel of bread in thine hand. And she said, As the LORD thy God liveth, I have not a cake, but an handful of meal in a barrel, and a little oil in a cruse: and, behold, I am gathering two sticks, that I may go in and dress it for me and my son, that we may eat it, and die. And Elijah said unto her, Fear not; go and do as thou hast said: but make me thereof a little cake first, and bring it unto me, and after make for thee and for thy son. For thus saith the LORD God of Israel, The barrel of meal shall not waste, neither shall the cruse of oil fail, until the day that the LORD sendeth rain upon the earth. And she went and did according to the saying of Elijah: and she, and he, and her house, did eat many days. And the barrel of meal wasted not, neither did the cruse of oil fail, according to the word of the LORD, which he spake by Elijah [1 KINGS 17:9-16]

A widow woman of Zarephath went to the city gate to gather fire wood to prepare her last meal for herself and her son, before they will die. At this particular moment in the city of Zarephath; so many lives had been lost because of the tendency of the famine. The widow woman had prayed and cried but her circumstances remained the same and she had; only a morsel of meal and little oil in a cruse left. The fear of death knocking had intimidated her household.

God answered her prayer by sending one of his ministers (Elijah) to her. Her answer was packaged upon her believing the prophet of God and acting upon his word without any atom of doubt. All that the woman needed was food that can sustain her family throughout the famine period.

Unfortunately the Prophet of God assigned to change her situation came to her with nothing. Absolutely nothing, not even a glass of water or slice of bread. Yet he carried the unction to sustain her family from death.

The prophet came to be fed by the Zarephath woman of what she has in her house. The man of God asked for a drink, and while she went in to fetch the water, he called her back and demanded for a meal. She truly confessed that the last meal in the house is meant for her and her son to eat and die. But the prophet declared unto her; fear not go and prepare me a meal first and there after make for yourself and your son.

Elijah said that the barrel of meal shall not waste. And according to the pronouncement of the prophet of God so it was to the widow woman that her last meal was supernaturally increased all the rest of her life and family through the liberation mandate of prophet.

THE BATTLE WINNING TICKET OF JERUSALEM

...Jehoshaphat stood and said, Hear me, O Judah, and ye inhabitants of Jerusalem; Believe in the LORD your God, so shall ye be established; believe his prophets, so shall ye prosper. [2 CHRONICLE 20:20]

Whenever Israel lost or failed to be led by sent ones among them they became victims of a wicked manoeuvring of their enemy. Three nations came against Judah but fortunately, they have the anointed agent of change among them. Their king inquired from the Lord God what they ought to do. And God spoke through the King to get ready the choristers and musicians, for the battle belongs to God if only they can trust in Him. So with the help of the spiritual leader, they experienced what I call sweat less victory.

NIGHT OF STRUGGLE TURNED TO A MIRACLE

Jesus declared that he has been anointed to heal the broken hearted In Luke gospel chapter 5. Simeon Peter toiled throughout the night as a professional fisherman but he came back frustrated. The result of his life was sour. He couldn't understand why despite his several years of experience in the fishing industry. There are so many people in the body of Christ whose life stories are a mystery they have no clue about. There comes a point that many give-up on themselves. Many become tired and hopeless in their dreams and visions being dashed to the will of their enemy.

Fortunately for Simon Peter the sent one showed up in his dark hour. May heaven show up in your dark moment in life. As Peter was about to go home to share the sad experience, Jesus asked for his ship to preach the good news and Simon willingly obliged him. Beloved what Simon offered as a matter of fact, was his personal life for Jesus to come into. The situation of his life still remained the same until Jesus gave him a command to launch out. He reluctantly obeyed the word of the anointed one and his life changed completely.

PETER AND JOHN AT THE BEAUTIFUL GATE

Now Peter and John were going up into the temple at the hour of prayer, [being] the ninth [hour]. And a certain man that was lame from his mother's womb was carried, whom they laid daily at the door of the temple which is called Beautiful, to ask alms of them that entered into the temple; who seeing Peter and John about to go into the temple, asked to receive alms. And Peter, fastening his eyes upon him, with John, said, Look on us. And he gave heed unto them, expecting to receive something from them. But Peter said, Silver and gold have I none; but what I have, that give I thee. In the name of Jesus Christ of Nazareth, walk. [ACTS 3:1-3]

The beggar at the beautiful gate asked for alms from the sent one. Peter and John knew what they carried. Not that they did not truly have money on them to give the beggar but they had the unction to actualize destinies. They told the beggar that they had no money to offer him but that there was something more than money. In the name of Jesus they released heaven's anointing that changed the beggar's life forever. There is always something that the anointed one carries. May you discover it so that you can recover your colourful destiny. By a prophet the Lord God delivered and by a prophet they were preserved. May heaven preserve your destiny!

CHAPTER FIVE

GOD'S AGENT FOR DIRECTION

I will raise them up a prophet from among their brethren, like unto thee, and will put my words in his mouth; and he shall speak unto them all that I shall command him
[DEUTERONOMY 18:18]

In life generally, there are some avenues for seeking direction especially in matters affecting ones destiny. God's way for mankind is the true way of living. It is He who created us. His way for our lives will give glory to him. Without his leading, there is nothing that will glorify His Name. His glory is the radiance of His splendour, the demonstration of his power and of course the atmosphere of His presence. Everything created by God reveals His Glory.

Yet he sent prophets to them, to bring them again unto the LORD; and they testified against them: but they would not give ear.
[2 CHRONICLES 24:19]

The use of human vessel by God is to give direction to man. Imagine a world you didn't create. You will certainly need someone to guide you. A world created by God, so we will need the leading of the prophet of God to give us divine direction. Take for example, a stranger arriving a city. He may trace or find his way through the city by following the directions provided in the city map. Also there are moments when our human senses are not required in most instances for success.

God is the only one who can provide true and absolutely dependable direction through life. For God to make this direction accessible to all, He has appointed apostles, Bishops, Pastors, Evangelist, Teachers to accomplish His will and to follow his ways because they are the best counsellors that we need.

Following God's direction means we are willing to pattern our lives after His own way. It implies that whoever He chooses is the best. His ways mean victory and success. His direction is destiny master key. He makes His way known to Moses and the children of Israel His acts.

God has made provisions for us to be directed. He uses several means to bring his direction to his people. One of these means is through His ministers. And there are so many blessings in following God's direction. We are assured of His backing and security.

But if thou shalt indeed obey his voice and do all that I speak; then I will be an enemy unto thine enemies an adversary unto thine adversaries **[EXODUS 23:22]**

You will not be in want whenever you allow the Lord to lead. God's directions are available to us daily as we walk with Him. It is not His will that we walk through life like people who are groping in darkness, unsure of what we are doing or where we are going.

They will ask for the way to Zion, turning their faces in its direction; they will come that they may join themselves to the LORD in an everlasting covenant that will not be forgotten.
[JEREMIAH 50:5]

THE REASON FOR HIS DIRECTION

- Everyone comes from God alone.

- Everyone lives unto Him knowingly or unknowingly.

- Everyone lives by His will.

- Everyone has His plan and purpose

- For His glory in our purpose.

- Everyone lives by His power

- You are created for Him and you are living for Him.

- You exist for His pleasure.

- He wants to take pleasure in your life.

- He is the author and finisher of our life.

Don't settle for just achieving the good life, because the good life is not good enough. You can have a lot to live on and still have nothing to live for.

GOD'S FOUNDATION

And are built upon the foundation of the apostles and prophets, Jesus Christ himself being the chief corner stone; in whom all the building fitly framed together growth unto a holy temple in the Lord. In whom ye also are builded together for a habitation of God through the Spirit. [EPHESIANS 2:20-22]

The stone which the builder rejected became the head of the corner. The foundation of the apostles and prophets is in conjunction with Christ Jesus. He came to do the will of God. He came to fulfil God's will and purpose. The Lord committed the doctrine of salvation, first to the prophets, Pastors, Evangelist, Teachers and then to the apostles. The end of which every matter of concern in life is tie to Christ and the chosen one. Therefore that is indeed the true and universal Church which is built upon Christ by the prophets and apostles, as a spiritual temple consecrated to God.

What is your foundation? Without a good foundation of a building, despite the colour or design or beauty such building is bound to fall.

DIVINE DIRECTION FOR THE WIFE OF THE LATE PROPHET

Now there cried a certain woman of the wives of the sons of the prophets unto Elisha, saying, Thy servant my husband is dead; and thou knowest that thy servant did fear the LORD:

***and the creditor is come to take unto him my
two sons to be bondmen. 2 Kings 4:1***

Science and technology has actually corrupted most believers
in looking at the manner of the world system in handling
their negative situation without seeking direction from God.
At every cross road of life God will always be pleased if we
could lean on him for directions. Lack of trust and confidence
on the spoken word of God has done too much harm and
damages to several destinies. A way that heaven cannot
make, no man can. We have lost absolute confidence in
believing our pastors even when we make enquiries from
them about God's direction over a given situation.

The only way a believer can be destroyed is only through
ignorance. To know the mind and the way of God in their
life is the key to walk into liberty and prosperity.

The prophet's wife facing bankruptcy and financial
indebtedness ran to the man of God for divine counselling.
The prophet Elijah asked her if there was still anything left
in her home and the woman said there was only one bottle
of oil. The man of God told her to go and borrow empty
vessels, so she quickly ran to her neighbours and borrowed
vessels. The woman and her son experienced miraculous
heaven supply of oil after confidently obeying the word of
the prophet.

***And Elisha said unto her, what shall I do for
thee? Tell me; what hast thou in the house? And
she said, Thy handmaid hath not anything in
the house, save a pot of oil. Then he said, go,***

borrow thee vessels abroad of all thy neighbours, even empty vessels; borrow not a few. And thou shalt go in, and shut the door upon thee and upon thy sons, and pour out into all those vessels; and thou shalt set aside that which is full. So she went from him, and shut the door upon her and upon her sons; they brought [the vessels] to her, and she poured out. And it came to pass, when the vessels were full, that she said unto her son, Bring me yet a vessel. And he said unto her, there is not a vessel more. And the oil stayed. Then she came and told the man of God. And he said, Go, sell the oil, and pay thy debt, and live thou and thy sons of the rest. 2 Kings 4: 2-7

CHAPTER SIX

MINISTER TO YOUR PASTOR

If we have sown unto you spiritual things, is it a great thing if we shall reap your carnal things? **[1 CORINTHIANS 9:11]**

Paul the apostle was responding to the often neglected truth concerning the Corinthian Church for not ministering to their spiritual ministers. Most believers know and do opt for what their pastors should do for them, but very few have the least knowledge of what their responsibilities are to their pastor. This kind of omission or neglect to the Church made the Apostle to ask the believers in Corinth *"if we have sown unto you spiritual things it is a great thing if we shall reap your carnal things?"*

Ministering to your pastor is a subject most pastors are very much silent about because it applies directly to them. Unfortunately, Paul makes us to know that others benefit from the blessing of the spiritual seed sown to a believers` while their minister is denied. If others be partakers of this power over you, are not we rather?

Nevertheless we have not used this power; but suffer all things, lest we should hinder the gospel of Christ. **[1 CORINTHIANS 9:11]**

If those who have served you in any matter have a right to a recompense for that service, surely we who have served you in the most essential matters have a right, but we have not availed ourselves of it, but have worked with our hands to bear our own charges, lest any of you should think that we preached the Gospel merely to procure a temporal support, and so be prejudiced against us, and thus prevent our success in the salvation of your souls.

The gospel of salvation through the name of our Lord and saviour Christ Jesus is the only hope to life. Regardless of the truth, the minister has a right to be supported for spiritual service rendered but they failed to do so in order not to hinder the preaching of the gospel. Today, most ministers of God all over the world are not able to minister effectively and efficiently because no one cares to minister to their needs.

The irony of the whole matter is that the kingdom business is hindered because most ministers are handicapped. The adversary taking advantage of this neglect has done numerous ills to most churches. Neglect on the part of the Jewish believers led to the priests abandoning their service at the Church to do other businesses or secular work to meet up their needs. This, Nehemiah strictly preached and taught about in order to have the pastor (priests) being restored back to their priesthood duties at the tabernacle.

We should take an immediate action to let leaders of churches and believers in this part of the world come to realize that Pastors working under churches are more important than the work they are doing. It is the Man of God first before the work of God.

The basic truth is that nobody can pay for the work ministers of God are doing; no matter the amount either in cash or in kind because it is God's work.

WHY THE NEGLECT?

LACK OF AWARENESS - *"....but suffer all things, lest we should hinder the gospel of Christ."* 1 CORINTHIANS **9:12**. Because the early priests failed to teach about their right to be ministered to avoid hindering the gospel. One thing that has made most pastors silent about this subject is because it applies directly to them. This is a great ignorance on the part of ministers.

NEGLECT - A few believers who know what to do, do little or nothing at all. While others feel that their pastor lacks nothing.

DYSFUNCTIONAL CHARACTER of some Christian leaders has also affected the interest of some believers. For instance, some leaders have been seen as men, who are greedy, covetous, they .amass wealth to themselves to the detriment of those working with them.

LACK OF SACRIFICE on the part of the believers

Most ministers of God carry a tremendous anointing in them because of the peculiarity of their divine calling. Supporting them under this kind of divine power directly provoke their angel to effect a positive change in your life.

You cannot invest, where you don't believe there is increase. Giving to support our pastor's needs is like sowing into a fertile ground. The anointing you bless will in turn bless you. God's word is no respecter of persons. God's word works for anyone who cares to obey it.

And it fell on a day, that Elisha passed to Shunem, where was a great woman; and she constrained him to eat bread. And so it was, that as oft as he passed by, he turned in thither to eat bread. And she said unto her husband, Behold now, I perceive that this is an holy man of God, which passeth by us continually. [2 KINGS 4:8]

This city was in the tribe of Issachar, to the south of the brook Kishon, and at the foot of Mount Tabor. Where was a great woman, this woman is said to have been the sister of Abishag, the Shunammite, well known in the history of David. The woman perceived that Elisha was a man of God, which means that the man of God wasn't her pastor. But she seized the opportunity in begging the prophet to come to her house. She constrained him to sow unto his life and support his ministry. Whatsoever you give to support men of God only leaves your hands but never leaves your life.

The Holy Spirit can help us release some seeds we are reluctant to release, only if we can be opened to His leading. The end result of the Shunammite woman giving unto the prophet provoked the anointing of the prophet to terminate the barrenness in her life.

Think about it, the pastor that always stands in the gap for you and your family in prayers, teaching, exhorting and counselling, all day, week, months and years and yet they have never eaten your bread or drank your water neither do you care to know the size of his shoes nor clothes.

Hear what the word says *"Thou shalt not muzzle the ox when he treadeth out the corn"* [DEUTERONMY 25:4] While the oxen were at work some muzzled their mouths to hinder them from eating the corn, which Moses here forbids, instructing the people by this symbolical precept to be kind to their servants and labourers, but especially to those who minister to them in holy things.

Also Apostle Paul emphasized it saying *"If we have sown unto you spiritual things, is it a great thing if we shall reap your carnal things?"* 1 CORINTHIANS 9:11. Through the spirit, Paul comparing the literal ox to the ministers of the gospel, asked the Corinthian brethren why they were negligent in their responsibilities to him.

Who serves as a soldier at his own expense? Who plants a vineyard and does not eat of its grapes? Who tends a flock and does not drink of the milk? Do I say this merely from a human point of view? NO. But we do not use this rightly. Rather, we put up with anything not to hinder the gospel of Christ.

WAYS OF SUPPORTING YOUR MINISTERS

PRAYERS – One of the most important areas to help your pastor is standing in prayer for him. Most of us never believe or know that we need to support our pastor through prayer and fasting. Why? Whenever your pastor is spiritually weak, it affects you. Because your destiny is connected to his spiritual success.

And it came to pass, when Moses held up his hand, that Israel prevailed: and when he let down his hand, Amalek prevailed. But Moses' hands were heavy; and they took a stone, and put it under him, and he sat thereon; and Aaron and Hur stayed up his hands, the one on the one side, and the other on the other side; and his hands were steady until the going down of the sun. **[EXODUS 17:11-12]**

His hands were steady; continued to be lifted up; showing that they felt that success must come from God. The servants of God may grow weary in prayer, and often they do so sooner than in the use of other means; but our great Advocate and Intercessor in heaven is never weary. Ministers of the gospel need the aid and encouragement of God's people through their prayers.

There is no inconsistency between healthy dependence on God, manifested in believing, affectionate, fervent prayer for blessings, and the most skilful, vigorous, and persevering use of all appropriate means to obtain them; but the proper use of the one secures and gives efficacy to the right performance of the other.

Jesus requested for prayer support from his disciples, but unfortunately they were all sleeping in the garden of Gethsemane. Also Apostle asked the Ephesians' brethren to pray for him.

FINANCIAL SUPPORT - We can give money to support our pastor and his family. The fact that they are spiritual men does not deny the fact that they are also human. Therefore we need to stand by them so that nothing can hinder them financially. For instance we notice that three women in Luke 8:1-3 ministered to Jesus of their substances, the shunammite woman in 2 Kings 4:8-10 gave prophet Elijah accommodation.

Make a decision today; stop being a receiver only but also a giver. You need to fulfil the agenda of God in giving to spread the gospel of salvation. Jesus, a perfect example, gave himself to the Father for salvation sake. Whatsoever you give promoting the gospel will certainly give you life.

Apostle Paul said not because I desire a gift: but I desire fruit that may abound to your account. Giving to men of God is your greatest hope for a better tomorrow. I've seen stagnated destinies released as the star by partnering with their pastors. But many are still blind in their minds to the cause of their limitations because they refuse to bless the anointed ones. Your pastor is your destiny.

CHAPTER SEVEN

PASTOR AND OTHER PASTORS

O ne of the most annoying attitudes of pastors is the spirit of strife and competing with one another. The great wall of division in the body of Christ has done so many harm to the Gospel of Our Lord.

But if ye have bitter jealousy and faction in your heart, glory not and lie not against the truth. This wisdom is not [a wisdom] that cometh down from above, but is earthly, sensual, and devilish. For where jealousy and faction are, there is confusion and every vile deed. [JAMES 3:14-16]

The church of Jesus is one body with various members functioning together to achieve its purpose. If this is true, why should one minister use the Church of God to discredit another man of God before the entire Church? He is afraid of the sheep of God going to the other pastor. If God truly called you why are you afraid? Shepherds never tie the sheep to take good care of them, the sheep willingly submit to his leading by trust. No Parent ties their children to feed. Those of you creating this mess and confusion should please stop corrupting the minds of the Lord's sheep.

We make ourselves judge the mode, form and the nature the Holy Spirit should move in the lives of other ministers.

If any minister of God goes above this level then we begin to talk evil and all manner of corrupt words to damage the minister credibility. If the minister is not up to our standard then they become also a subject of ridicule.

TOUCH NOT MY ANOINTED

Touch not mine anointed, and do my prophets no harm. **[PSALM 105:15]**

To Some men of God, they live as if they are excluded from the above warning in the word of God. Whatsoever is written is written for all.

Pastor Sir, be careful not to stain your anointing by wrong relationship and conduct to other servants of the Most High God like yourself. We know in part and so let us prophecy in part. No one had the right to judge but to pray for one another. Aaron was supposed to receive the anointing from Moses but it was Joshua the son of Nun who eventually did. The ignorant ones lose their ministries and anointing like Saul. The end result of this satanic manipulation is blaspheming, slandering and mocking other men of God at the expense of the success of their callings. Saul attempted to kill David several times but God stood to protect him. David got the opportunity to kill Saul but he refused simply because Saul was anointed by God. Beloved, learn and applied wisdom and divine understanding. David applied divine wisdom to maintain his anointing when he heard of the death of Saul and his Son. David declares to Israel,

"Tell it not in Gath, Proclaim it not in the streets of Ashkelon-Lest the daughters of the Philistines rejoice, Lest the daughters of the uncircumcised triumph". **[2 SAMUEL 1:20]**

The word of the Lord demanded that we should walk in love with one another. Don't not celebrate the wrongs or errors of men of God but to show them love in prayer and giving. Mike Murdock ones said *"what you make happened for others, God will make happened for you."*

The Bible declares that

"Henceforth, let no man trouble me; for I bear in my body the marks of the Lord Jesus".
[GALATIANS 6:17]

Beloved it is too risky to pass derogatory statements about men of God. Let us stop criticizing one another. The reason why so many ministries and churches are crawling today is because of this. The harvest for criticizing is stagnation. Thank God for his divine knowledge revealed in this book in saving lives, churches and ministries from this demonic cancer that has destroyed others. There is so much envy amongst us. Let us look unto Him who has called us. I got no heaven of my own that I want my members to go; except the only one the scripture tells us about. Let us render our service to God in truth and sincerity of heart, in reverence to the living God so that we may be able to depart from all form of evil work.

The devil is your enemy. Stop fighting other ministries with your tongue. In most Christian cities today, so many wrong things are going on within the body of Christ.

Pastors, stop fighting other pastors because of church members. Please be reminded that the number of Church members doesn't determine your eternity with God. But it is regarded as heaven determining factor to see whether you feed the sheep or care after them as it is required of a true shepherd. If not, it is written that hell is wide open but makes your choice not to go there.

Most mega Church pastors never believe or accept other pastors that they were called by God. You should not judge any man simply because of the spiritual leadership you have. Fight your ways at the level of humility because anointing that is abused can be taken away. May your anointing be kindled with fire forever more.

Life and death is in the power of the tongue. Respect heavenly order and authority for there is no other power except the power from above. There is no age limit or barrier to the anointing.

Workers in the church of God depart from all forms of evil. Don't destroy your destiny. If the privilege of working closely with your pastor could make you loose your focus from his anointing; please save your soul and move to other department in the Church. It is too dangerous to allow your pastor's weakness to lure you into gossip and side talk. Gehazi destroyed his destiny and his descendant with leprosy whilst serving the prophet of God. Judas destroyed his colourful ministry and died by hanging himself on a tree after he betrayed his master. It is too costly to toy with Gods altar of fire.

DANGER OF OFFENCES

Woe unto the world because of offences! For it must needs be that offences come; but woe to that man by whom the offence cometh!
[MATTHEW 18:7]

From the above scripture Jesus stated that offences will surely come. But cursed is that man by whom the offence comes.

John the Baptist was beheaded by Herod because he was offended by Jesus not coming to the prison to see him. Here is the word of Jesus as declare in **MATTHEW 11:4-6**

"Jesus answered and said to them, "Go and tell John the things which you hear and see. The blind see and the lame walk; the lepers are cleansed and the deaf hear; the dead are raised up and the poor have the gospel preached to them. And blessed is he who is not offended because of Me."

"And Simeon blessed them, and said unto Mary his mother, Behold, this [child] is set for the falling and the rising of many in Israel; and for a sign which is spoken against" **[LUKE 1:34]**

When Jesus was brought to the temple for dedication; this was the proclamation made on him as God sent prophet to the world. That many lives and destinies will rise and fulfil their purpose on earth while many will fall under a curse and closed heaven. Every true minister of God has this unction over their anointing.

As a result of this, God by himself brought Miriam under a curse when she murmured against Moses. When Miriam despised Moses; the sent one, Moses did not even hear it but God heard it. Do not be deceived beloved because your pastor didn't hear or know anything you said about him. Forget about pastor hearing or not hearing but if you believe God heard it, know that you have brought a curse upon your life.

> *And the anger of Jehovah was kindled against them; and he departed. And the cloud removed from over the Tent; and, behold, Miriam was leprous, as [white as] snow: and Aaron looked upon Miriam, and, behold, she was leprous.*
> **[NUMBER 12:9-10]**

Moses had to use his office as the heaven ambassador to intercede for Miriam to be forgiven. God listened to his prophet and forgive her.

The wife of David, Michal touched the anointed one, her own husband David. Remember the book of **ACTS 2:29-30** clearly states that David was not just a King but he was also a prophet of God. David excitement and joy made him dance at the temple the day the ark of God was brought back into the city.

> *And it was so, as the ark of Jehovah came into the city of David that Michal the daughter of Saul looked out at the window, and saw King David leaping and dancing before Jehovah; and she despised him in her heart.* **[2 SAMUEL 6:16]**

Then David returned to bless his household. And Michal

the daughter of Saul came out to meet David, and said, how glorious was the king of Israel to-day, who uncovered himself to-day in the eyes of the handmaids of his servants, as one of the vain fellows shamelessly uncovered himself. **[2 SAMUEL 6:20]**

God watched over his word to perform it. He saw and heard Saul daughter who was David's Wife, because God is not respecter of person, Michal brought a curse of barrenness to her life. In fact she was the only woman in the Bible that was barren.

So many people destiny may be under this same curse of barrenness and stagnation. Unfruitfulness in jobs, business and career, is as a result of barrenness.

I have been anointed to break every curse. Pray this prayer sincerely from your heart. Lord Jesus has mercy on me. I confess all my sins before you today. Sins of murmuring, foolish talks and despising of your prophets. I repent today; cleanse me with your blood. Thank you for your forgiveness in Jesus name, Amen.

By the power and the anointing of God upon my life, I therefore declare you free from the power of darkness. You shall experience reward, breakthrough, and fruitfulness in Jesus Name.

Arise and shine for the glory of the Lord has risen upon you. You will be celebrated. Receive lifting in your destiny. Receive increase in your finances. Rise and possess your possession. Whatsoever the cankerworms and caterpillars have eaten I command a double and speedy restoration now in Jesus name.

Shall the prey be taken from the mighty, or the lawful captives be delivered? But thus saith Jehovah, Even the captives of the mighty shall be taken away, and the prey of the terrible shall be delivered; for I will contend with him that contendeth with thee, and I will save thy children. And I will feed them that oppress thee with their own flesh; and they shall be drunken with their own blood, as with sweet wine: and all flesh shall know that I, Jehovah, am thy Saviour, and thy Redeemer, the Mighty One of Jacob. **[ISAIAH 49:24-26]**

This is your season. Be refreshed and renewed from today.

There are many churches but few Pastors

LOOK UNTO GOD AND NOT MEN

It is so disgraceful to see anointed men and women losing their focus from above. God has never given a vision without provision. God is not author of confusion. As soldiers of the cross, we should be ready to fight the fight of faith in fulfilling our calling. Every called one has a battle to fight in standing for the truth. The scripture which is the mind of God in helping to give shape and colour to society has long been abandoned and neglected. Jesus is a perfect example for men and women to emulate. He suffered rejection, accused of blasphemy, of being man but made himself to be equal with God.

The failure to make God our absolute fortress results in divine disconnection. You shall know the truth, and the truth will make you free from the power of darkness that have cover the whole earth.

Give none offence, neither to the Jews, nor to the Gentiles, nor to the church of God.
[1 CORINTHIANS 10:32]

Giving no offence in anything that the ministry is not blamed. [2 CORINTHIANS 6:3]

Any ministry can receive the wrath of God when it fails to guide against offence. Give no room to the devil to deceive you.

HOW TO PROVOKE THE ANOINTING FOR BLESSING

GIVE THEM HONOUR - *"And they were offended in him. But Jesus said unto them, A prophet is not without honour, save in his own country, and in his own house. Render therefore to all their dues: tribute to whom tribute is due; custom to whom custom; fear to whom fear; honour to whom honour.* [ROMANS 13:7]

What regards do we have for them? Do we truly respect them as God's servant? Beloved, we need to develop an attitude of reverence unto them because of the special place they have with God. The respect you give to men of God should be more than the honour we give to our boss in the office. Men of God are worthy of much more honour than presidents of nations. They are spiritual watchmen over nations and lives.

Irrespective of your grey hair or your educational background, it is a divine wisdom to honour and respect them because degree or age is irrelevant in the realm of the spirit. We are not controlled by the world standard, but by the word of God. Life is more spiritual that is why degree and big grammar have not been able to free anyone in the world today.

PRAY FOR THEM - *Brethren, pray for us.* **1THESSALONIANS 5:25.** Apostle Paul asked the brethren to remember them in prayers so that their calling to serve the believers will be faithfully delivered. You can provoke the anointing upon your man of God by standing in prayer for them and their family. Whenever the shepherd is removed, the sheep will scatter. Unfortunately, many believers do not know that their pastors need their spiritual support in prayers. Jesus requested for prayers from his disciples, sadly enough they were all sleeping in the Garden of Gethsemane. A church that does not pray for their pastor who is standing in the gap for them against the forces of the wicked ones is a sleeping church.

Moses hands were being strengthened in the place of prayer as soon as they discovered that he was weak. His weakness automatically gave the philistines great opportunities for their advancement to the territory of the camp of the Israelites. **[EXODUS 17:10-14]**

When your pastor is spiritually weak, it affects you. This is because your success and destiny is directly or indirectly tied to how much of heaven anointing working in your spiritual life.

And on my behalf, that utterance may be given unto me in opening my mouth, to make known with boldness the mystery of the gospel, for which I am an ambassador in chains; that in it I may speak boldly, as I ought to speak.
[EPHESIANS 6:18-20]

Apostle Paul asked the Ephesians church to pray for him so that his mouth will open to speak the word of life with boldness under the leading and the empowerment of the Holy Ghost as he ought to speak. Pray for your pastor in the same manner for more unction to function, for divine wisdom, boldness, strength, courage. When the fire over his life is still burning every wicked force that makes any attempt on your life and family will be consumed.

TESTIMONY

Few years back one of my daughters in the Church shared this testimony: She saw in her dream evil men dressed like Doctors giving some other people injection. When they got to her, she refused the injection and they asked her if Doctor Lawrence is her Doctor, she said yes and immediately she woke up.

When we lack the divine covering of the sent one we become vulnerable to every wicked manoeuvring of the devil.

MINISTER TO THEM IN CASH AND KIND - *He that received you received me, and he that received me received him that sent me. He that received a* *prophet in the name of a prophet shall receive a prophet's reward: and he that received a righteous man in the name of a righteous man shall receive a righteous man's reward. And whosoever shall give to drink unto one of these little ones a cup of cold water only, in the name of a disciple, verily I say unto you he shall in no wise lose his reward.* [MATTHEW 10:40-42]

There is a spark of glory that follows those who have a covenant in giving to support their men of God. Do this with all humility and not in pride. Give whatsoever you are led to give by the spirit of God, do it willing.

You cannot give what you do not have. The Zeraphath widow woman gave her little to Prophet Elijah and she got the blessing of God upon the little meal left in her house. She survived the famine and the credit crunch.

Today, many folks in churches are using all manner of tricks to ask for money, shoe, chocolate, etc from their pastor whom they are supposed to bless with their substance.

Now therefore restore the man his wife; for he is a prophet, and he shall pray for thee, and thou shalt live. [GENESIS 20:7]

Abraham received men that he blessed for a special menu without knowing that he was honouring and provoking the blessing over these men's lives. Abraham was feeding the angel of God without knowing. Soon after the angel had eaten; they asked for his wife Sarah who was right in the living room; they declared to Abraham that Sarah his wife will conceive and bear a son at the same time next year.

Nobody can pay for the work that the ministers of God are doing; no matter how big the amount may be. It is God's work and only God alone can pay for it.

> *For it was so, when Jezebel cut off the prophets of the LORD, that Obadiah took an hundred prophets, and hid them by fifty in a cave, and fed them with bread and water.* **[1 KINGS 18:4]**

CHAPTER EIGHT

PASTORS AS SPIRITUAL FATHERS

For though ye have ten thousand instructors in Christ, yet have ye not many fathers: for in Christ Jesus I have begotten you through the gospel. [1 CORINTHIANS 4:15]

And I will give you pastors according to mine heart, which shall feed you with knowledge and understanding. [Jeremiah 3:15]

Father is a gift from God. Not every man of God is a father. No one chooses his biological father by himself. Likewise it is God that needs to choose our spiritual father for us. The Bible says in JEREMIAH 3:15 *"that God will give us a spiritual father in accordance to his own heart that will feed us with his knowledge and understanding"*.

Apostle Paul pointed out to the Corinthians church that not all the visiting preachers were fathers. For though ye have ten thousand instructors in Christ, yet have ye not many fathers. Many may impact your life but they are not fathers.

CHARACTERISTICS OF A FATHER

- A Father is concerned about his children's welfare

- He makes plans in advance for their care

- He loves the presence of his children always

- A father's love never departs from his children

- He gives directions and protects them from harm

- Fathers are committed and patient

- They take full responsibility

THERE ARE SEVERAL TYPES OF FATHER:

YOUR HEAVENLY FATHER - *"When ye pray, say Our Father which art in heaven"* LUKE **11:2**. Our heavenly father loves and cares for our life more than we can ever imagine. He owns the plans for our life. Without Him, we will not be in existence. He loves us so much that He sent his only begotten Son from heaven to pay for our sins.

YOUR BIOLOGICAL FATHER - This is the father from whose seed you were born. This is the only father that you can truly recognize physically as a father. But this is a mistake because God will send a father into your life to make a positive difference that can change one's life forever. Our biological father has a responsibility to train the child from infancy to adulthood.

YOUR FATHER IN CHRIST - This is the person who brought you to the Lord, or the person who birth you into the ministry of the Lord. Through him you find yourself involved in the work of the Kingdom of God.

Your Father-in-Law - Now Moses kept the flock of Jethro his father's in-law. There are many father in-laws who have been a great inspiration to their sons' in-law.

Step Father - This type of father often replaces the biological father. Step father emanates in life as a result of the unavailability of biological father either because of death, divorce, abandonment or remarriage.

Father of Faith - Know ye therefore that they which are of faith, the same are the children of Abraham **[Galatians 3:7]**. Fathers are special but the son may do greater than a father yet a father is always a father.

> *"Honour thy father and thy mother so that thy days may be long upon the land which the Lord thy God giveth thee"* **[Exodus 20:12]**

Fathers have the power to bless and to curse. We need to honour them in order for us to receive their blessings and not curses. Fathers occupy a special seat of authority given to them by the Lord in impacting the lives of their children. We should learn the importance of this very position of our fathers in the fulfilment of our destiny. Any kind of father assigned to you by God is an authority in your life.

There is a tremendous power released when a father speaks a blessing over a son.

> *"A son honoureth his father and a servant his master: if then I be a father, where is mine*

honour? And if I be a master, where is my fear? saith the LORD of hosts unto you, O priests, that despise my name. And ye say, wherein have we despised thy name" [MALACHI 1:6]

Chapter Nine

Biblical Caution for Pastors

B ut the prophet, who shall presume to speak a word in my name, which I have not commanded him to speak, or that shall speak in the name of other gods, even that prophet shall die.

When a prophet speaketh in the name of the LORD, if the thing follow not, nor come to pass, that is the thing which the LORD hath not spoken. [DEUTERONOMY 18:22]

The priests said not, Where is Jehovah? and they that handle the law knew me not: the rulers also transgressed against me, and the prophets prophesied by Baal, and walked after things that do not profit. Wherefore I will yet contend with you, saith Jehovah, and with your children's children will I contend. For pass over to the isles of Kittim, and see; and send unto Kedar, and consider diligently; and see if there hath been such a thing. Hath a nation changed [its] gods, which yet are no gods? But my people have changed their glory for that which doth not profit. Be astonished, O ye heavens, at this, and be horribly afraid, be ye very desolate, saith Jehovah. [JEREMIAH 2:8-12]

Woe is me because of my hurt! My wound is grievous: but I said, truly this is [my] grief, and I must bear it. My tent is destroyed, and all my cords are broken: my children are gone forth from me, and they are not: there is none to spread my tent any more, and to set up my curtains. For the shepherds are become brutish, and have not inquired of Jehovah: therefore they have not prospered, and all their flocks are scattered. [JEREMIAH 10:19-22]

The wind shall eat up all thy pastors, and thy lovers shall go into captivity: surely then shalt thou be ashamed and confounded for all thy wickedness. [JEREMIAH 22:22]

Woe be unto the pastors that destroy and scatter the sheep of my pasture! saith Therefore thus saith the LORD God of Israel against the pastors that feed my people; Ye have scattered my flock, and driven them away, and have not visited them: behold, I will visit upon you the evil of your doings, saith the LORD. [JEREMIAH 23:1-2]

And I have seen folly in the prophets of Samaria. [JEREMIAH 23:13]

I have seen also in the prophets of Jerusalem an horrible thing: they commit adultery, and walk in lies: they strengthen also the hands of evildoers, that none doth return from his wickedness: they are all of them unto me as Sodom, and the inhabitants thereof as Gomorra. [JEREMIAH 23:14]

I have not sent these prophets, yet they ran: I have not spoken to them, yet they prophesied.
[JEREMIAH 23:21]

I have heard what the prophets said, that prophesy lies in my name, saying, I have dreamed, I have dreamed.   [JEREMIAH 23:25]

How long shall this be in the heart of the prophets that prophesy lies? yea, they are prophets of the deceit of their own heart;
[JEREMIAH 23:26]

Therefore, behold, I am against the prophets, saith the LORD, that steal my words everyone from his neighbour.   [JEREMIAH 23:30]

Behold, I am against the prophets, saith the LORD, that use their tongues, and say, He saith.
[JEREMIAH 23:31]

And mine hand shall be upon the prophets that see vanity, and that divine lies: they shall not be in the assembly of my people; neither shall they be written in the writing of the house of Israel, neither shall they enter into the land of Israel; and ye shall know that I am the Lord GOD.   [EZEKIEL 13:9]

Your fathers, where are they? and the prophets, do they live forever?   [ZECHARIAH 1:5]

But my words and my statutes, which I commanded my servants the prophets, did they not take hold of your fathers? and they returned and said, Like as the LORD of hosts thought to do unto us, according to our ways, and according to our doings, so hath he dealt with us. [ZECHARIAH 1:6]

And many false prophets shall rise, and shall deceive many. [MATTHEW 24:11]

For there shall arise false Christ's, and false prophets, and shall shew great signs and wonders; insomuch that, if it were possible, they shall deceive the very elect.
[MATTHEW 24:24]

And are built upon the foundation of the apostles and prophets, Jesus Christ himself being the chief corner stone. [EPHESIANS 2:20]